Healing Mind

5 Steps to Ultimate Healing, 4 Rooms for Thoughts:
Achieve Satisfaction Through a Well Managed Mind

Janice McDermott, M.Ed., LCSW

Foreword by
C. Norman Shealy, MD, PhD

BALBOA.
PRESS
A DIVISION OF HAY HOUSE

Balboa Press books may be ordered through booksellers or by contacting:

Balboa Press
A Division of Hay House
1663 Liberty Drive
Bloomington, IN 47403
www.balboapress.com
1 (877) 407-4847

Cover art: St. Louis, Missouri, artist Sharon Spillar (Spillar Studios, LLC, http://www.spillarstudio.com) granted permission to use a copy of the painting *Think Tank*.

Unless otherwise indicated, all Scripture quotations are from The King James Version of The Holy Bible by Public Domain.

Print information available on the last page.

ISBN: 978-1-5043-3701-4 (sc)
ISBN: 978-1-5043-3700-7 (hc)
ISBN: 978-1-5043-3702-1 (e)

Library of Congress Control Number: 2015911348

Balboa Press rev. date: 07/24/2015

To my grandchildren:
Christopher, Anna, and Jack

CONTENTS

ACKNOWLEDGMENTS

Margery Williams's classic tale *The Velveteen Rabbit or How Toys Become Real*, written in 1922 when she was in her forties, captures the concept of becoming real in a simple, wonderful story, of which only a small portion is included here.

Melissa Reynolds, LCSW, a former social work student, motivated me to complete this project after the beautiful people in the recovery community insisted that I write it.

My son, Timothy, encouraged me repetitively with, "You can do it, Mom."

Moreover, to my proofreaders, who wish to remain anonymous, and to St. Louis artist Sharon Spillar for the cover art (Spillar Studios, LLC, http://www.spillarstudio.com), thank you.

FOREWORD

Some books are for education, some for self-therapy, and some for deep healing. *Healing Mind* is intended for all these purposes and more. It is for deep thinking and deep personal work for ultimate healing. Although Janice emphasizes much of the great contributions of Carl Jung, she starts with the most critical need for most people—learning to experience their physical feelings, those unrecognized and forgotten reactions to hurt, especially those they've blocked, the ones Wilhelm Reich called "armoring." Indeed, he said, among other things, that he had never seen a Westerner with an unlocked pelvis. In other words, we hide our unresolved stress in muscle tension, especially in the pelvis and sexual aspects of life.

Ultimately, it is your unfulfilled need for healthy nurturing and your fear of being harmed that began the armoring process. A majority of individuals never overcome the feelings that prevent them from living happy, productive lives. The time has come to retire the critic, who sabotages your well-being.

Healing Mind provides you with a workbook—indeed a fun playbook—to release the unfinished anger, guilt, anxiety, and sadness that have been blocking your inner Child. Here are tools for your wise Mentor to use to nurture you to full mental and physical health and to awaken your Divine Child. Enter these four enchanting rooms with eager anticipation of a happy journey.

C. Norman Shealy, MD, PhD
Founder and CEO, National Institute of Holistic Medicine
Author of *Living Bliss—*
Major Developments along the Holistic Path

INTRODUCTION

By changing our thinking processes, we can create a rich and fulfilling inner life that then manifests a rich and satisfying outer life. For most of us, what was missing as children is still missing for us today. We recreate the form of our childhood through all our relationships, as perceived when we were under six years old (not necessarily the content but definitely the form). Why would we do this? Because we are following an inherited subconscious map. If we needed rescuing from abuse, loneliness, confusion as young children, unless we have done extensive psychological work, we still need what was, and is, missing. We are all on a quest to heal the form, to fix what is broken, to find what is missing, and to create a perfect world for ourselves—heaven on earth, the paradise imagined.

In part one, we begin the process of building a foundation by becoming our own therapists, by acquiring the insight and skills the most competent therapists use to help achieve inner peace, self-confidence, and self-love. People who get what they want know how to love themselves. Your clutter-filled mind, clogged with questions, confusion, criticism, and mental fatigue, builds internal pressure that now can become peaceful, calm, and organized as you take control and build a foundation of internal support.

Next, armed with information and skills, we advance to part two, whereby we build our internal structure for creating what every satisfied person has—a well-organized mind. By using four of our culturally acquired Judeo-Christian archetypes, we become architects. We study the provided blueprint, gather our materials, and build our four rooms of mind. Moreover, when we finish, we will find that our sense of compassion, self-love, and acceptance has become greater than the sum of these parts. We gift ourselves through this process with an abundance of creativity and Spirituality, the way we were always meant to be. Therefore, "make yourself what you want the world to become" (Mohandas Gandhi).

PART I

THE JOURNEY

Uncomfortable things happen to all of us on our journey to becoming real.; as we drop our facade and allow our authentic self to shine in the presence of others. My journey, though I didn't recognize it as such at the time, began with an unfamiliar internal rumble the news of my father's unexpected death in 1973 initiated. The first time I knowingly set becoming real as a goal was ten years later in 1983 at the Esalen Institute in Big Sur, California.

My anxiety, years of built up childhood fear, was going through the roof in anticipation of my turn on the hot seat. Each participant of the three-sessions-a-day, weeklong workshop randomly took a turn sitting in the hot seat in the center of the circle. The one in the hot seat listened as each member, in turn, commented on his or her experience with the person in the center. I was the last one. I revealed that in the past ten years since my father's death, I had been divorced, had married again, and was now in the process of my second divorce. My internal rumble had become an earthquake. I hurt but didn't cry; I was ugly when I cried. I didn't show emotions in public. As I listened to each comment in turn, I became aware that even with fifteen sets of eyes observing me, no one saw me.

Having participated in relating anxiety-laden stories in groups, taking hot spring baths, and getting massages, I hadn't revealed anything. I was imprisoned by my body armor built by all the difficulties of childhood.

How did I get this way? All I was sure of was that I was afraid and that I had been hiding in the role of a good participant, which hadn't turned out very well. I began intense work to discover what lay beneath my fears. Who am I? How do I express my inner being? Answering these questions became for me a Spirit-directed journey using this process I'm sharing with you. The following stories will give you an idea of how I became so untrue to myself.

Each of us has childhood events that set us on a course of armoring ourselves against the world. Mining our childhood memories helps us discover the answers to how, when, and why we hide ourselves against the world. Even the most incidental childhood memory holds a treasure of information as evidenced by our remembering. Our real self lies under all the layers of physical armor build out of fear and others' expectations. We must remove this body armor layer by layer until we reach what is authentic, all our talents and spontaneous creative energy.

My earliest childhood memories begin in the middle of the Second World War. On Sundays, we attended service at a large Christian church. I remember being three years old and standing with five or six other children in front of a large congregation, awaiting my turn to say the Bible verse: "All we like sheep have gone astray" (Isa 53:6). When my turn came, I said, "All we like sheep have gone astray. Leave them alone, and they'll come home, wagging their tails behind them." Everyone laughed; cementing in my mind that church was a fun place.

My father was an airplane mechanic in the manufacturing division of the Ford Willow Run facility, which was a bomber aircraft plant in Michigan during WWII. He built heavy bombers, the B-24 Liberator. Knowing that all the construction teams were "learn as you go" people made him literally sick to his stomach with fear when he once had to fly to another city as part of his job. This was the only time I ever saw him sick. (Two weeks before his death, he made an enjoyable flight to Hawaii.) He modeled wellness and how to hide one's shortcomings for me.

An embellished education history and tenacity for survival through hard work secured him many jobs not usually afforded those with only a sixth-grade education and an inability to spell even the simplest words. Until his death at fifty-nine, he hid his embarrassment of not having an education and prided himself on his problem-solving abilities, math skills, good posture, ideal weight, and strength. He could outthink and outwork the next person and took pride in having the prettiest farm with the straightest fences in the county. Dr. C. Norman Shealy would describe him as living a "conscientious" life. From my father I learned perseverance and gained an appreciation for symmetry. In addition I learned to conceal my less admirable characteristics by unknowingly restricting my diaphragm.

By 1943 my family, along with hundreds of wives and children of servicemen, lived in Louisville, Kentucky, in the rows and rows of two-story yellow cinder block buildings, which had little to no grass, trees, or flowers and only one large asphalt playground for about two hundred or so children of all ages. At that time, government housing was a benefit afforded those whose fathers were involved in the war or war projects. Somehow, I was more privileged than other children were. My daddy was the only daddy coming home at night because he was building airplanes. However, I didn't mention that fact then because the other children wouldn't have liked me (maybe my mother told me that part), and I kept myself in fear through the imagery of his leaving. I built another layer of armor through tension in my shoulders.

The atmosphere in the housing project was always one of fear and foreboding. We were all trapped, waiting for that dreaded knock at the door that announced death; in turn it would necessitate a move for the remaining family members. Fear was so pervasive that I thought I could reach out and touch it, even though I was too young to know what it meant. I imagined it as a black fog rolling in to take the life right out of us when we least expected it—a real boogeyman. I saw the world as a dangerous, life-threatening place. Hence, I became forever hypervigilant and less trusting, a fear point on the Enneagram of personality types, more layers of armor.

My brother, two and a half years younger, was born in Louisville. His arrival changed my status from "only" to "oldest," a new role. Roles are evidence of armoring and serve to restrict our spontaneity. I became over responsible through self-denial.

I had to look out for my little brother, even more so after my father was drafted. Although Dad was deaf in his left ear since birth, the army still wanted him. My father's departure for boot camp at Fort Seal, Oklahoma, and the rationing of meat, sugar, and rubber increased my mother's fear, creating a domino effect in my brother and me. Our parents' fears become our own. My mother, raised with access to all the candy she wanted from her father's grocery, perceived a limited supply of sugar as a real security threat. She responded by keeping one hundred pounds of sugar in an army footlocker. Once when we were traveling by train as we made the move to Louisville, a train porter, noting the weight of the trunk, asked, "What do you have in here, lady? Pure gold?"

She replied, "That's right, pure gold." Her hand quickly reached around to cover my mouth, preventing me from saying, "No, it's sugar."

She'd acquired sugar by trading her meat ration stamps for sugar stamps. We could get meat without stamps from my uncle, who worked as a butcher but we didn't talk about that. My throat muscles took on a stiffness.

The war was over before my father finished boot camp. He returned home from training, unannounced, with a big box of Mounds candy bars for my mother. She placed the box atop the refrigerator to be doled out little by little. My body felt the release of long held anxiety with my father's return and that release became associated with chocolate. From that point on, chocolate and sugar could make anything feel better.

Now that my father no longer worked for the government, we were required to move from government housing. Even though we relocated, fear wouldn't remain behind. It had filled all the space around the cells in my body, the epigenetic home of my cellular memories. Our body remembers what our mind forgets.

My whole family left Louisville behind—and with it our car, for the tires had deteriorated. There were no tire replacements for several years due to the rubber shortage from the war. At his new job in Independence, Virginia, my father worked nights on an assembly line, making women's stockings. This was a big change from building airplanes. With the return of so many men and their flooding the job market, my father once again portrayed himself as a high school graduate. However, by doing so, his greatest real-self ability, learning quickly through hands-on experience, wasn't acknowledged. He did whatever it took to get himself hired; he was always hired. The lesson for me was act in your own behalf and don't expect others to save you from life's circumstance. The "toughen-up" armor appeared across my chest to protect my heart.

I liked living in the Blue Ridge Mountains. They gave me a sense of protection as they wrapped the horizon in every direction. Nature became my foundation of hope. There were new things to play with and do. We made apple cider in the fall and watched little snowballs become giants as they rolled down the mountain for my dad then to stack into a snowman. My brother and I lay in our beds, piled high with colorful handmade quilts while listening to the mountain stories visitors told in the next room. We rode in the horse-drawn wagon over the mountain. We chased chickens and each other. I could run as far as I wanted and laugh as loudly as I liked. My real self grew. Fear didn't live in these mountains.

After a year and a half, my father followed his passion, which was to create a showplace from the farm and house in western Kentucky, where he'd been born. Moving back to Kentucky took a day and part of a night. The moving truck carried our furniture and us. My father and brother rode in the back, with our collie by their side and our two pet chickens in a coup. My mother and I kept the driver company. The message was to follow your heart's desire no matter what is happening around you.

Unlike Virginia country living, Kentucky country was a struggle for me. When we struggle, we hold tension in our bodies. Long held tension becomes armor. The environment was a little scary but exciting, elements of anxiety. The three-room house had a sweeping front porch with blackberry thickets, which crawled up and around the walls, and a yard teeming with copperhead snakes and rabbits. For the first time in my young years, there was no electricity or indoor plumbing. A galvanized washtub filled with water to warm in the sun became our bathtub. I felt exposed bathing in the yard.

It took a year for my father to clear the land. By this time, the TVA (Tennessee Valley Authority) had provided electricity and sprayed the houses and barns with DDT. The remodeling of the house, while we lived in it, took another year. A tarp over my bed was all that kept the rain out while the roof was being redesigned.

My father taught me life skills—to watch out for snakes, to distinguish a bull calf from a heifer calf, to raise baby chickens, and to know which animals we would eat or sell. I learned where and when to be attached and how to let go and grieve. I created mental and emotional boundaries. I learned to do what my daddy did to survive in the world. I armored myself even further. I hid my shortcomings (dyslexia being one) and acted bravely. I was pleased with my attunement with nature and my common sense. I felt like a native Indian.

At six I was very much aware of the Spiritual forms of life around me and the world of things unseen. Having no other living ancestors, other than a few aunts and uncles who lived too far to visit more than once every few years, I identified with my father's deceased Native American grandmother, as I imagined her. Her presence was a constant companion due to the isolation that forced me inward to an imaginary world of others. Her Spirit seemed to dwell just over my left shoulder. My connection with the Spirit world, though I never discussed it, seemed normal. I thought everyone had my experience. I found comfort in the silence of my mind through nature and my grandmother's Spiritual presence. She remained with me until I was fifty-two, departing at my mother's funeral. This became my avenue of strength and self confidence.

One memory stands out from that time on the farm. A red and white baby calf died two days after birth and remained stretched out for a whole day behind our barn, looking perfect in every way. Magical thinking served me well as a child. I believed that with enough concentration and faith, I would be able to perform miracles like Jesus. I could be Spiritually powerful.

Unaware of the finality of death, I sat beside the dead calf for half a day, wishing and praying, "Dear Jesus, please let the baby calf breathe and stand up." I expected that at any moment the calf would rise to its feet, alive. I could see myself clapping my hands, overjoyed, a hero. Time passed, the day grew warmer, and heat waves rose from the corpse of the calf. Magic was happening, and I was present to it. I could feel the glory of it inside me. Awesome!

After a while, my young perception began to understand that the waves were the calf's life leaving its body. I thought, *This calf decided to go back to heaven, and so can I. I don't have to stay here. I can leave any time.* After that, I imagined many times in the silence of the forest and in the dark of the night that my Spirit rose like heat waves to soar with the angels and dance among the stars. I didn't know that I was learning to read the energy vibrations of living things, a tool that all healers use.

By the time I was nine, my parents expected my brother and me to employ our learned survival skills, to achieve a level of independent living, ready or not. We worked in the garden, picked strawberries to earn money, did farm chores, and worked, worked, and worked ... from sunup until sundown. Play was the work we liked: feeding the cats, planting peanuts, and gathering eggs. Attending church, going to vacation Bible school, and occasionally visiting my aunt (my mother's sister) every year or so for a week were our entertainment. My sister was born when I was nine, and another sister was born eighteen months later. While my parents focused on my younger siblings, my brother and I were on our own.

I remember visiting with my aunt for a week at her sister-in-law's home. For the first time in my life, I had a large bedroom to myself. I stood in front of a tall, freestanding, full-length mirror to admire myself in my first pink, silky-feeling nightgown. Sewn to the right side was a round-cord tie belt. I tied it around my waist and could see in the mirror that one end of the cord was a lot longer than the other. I contemplated cutting it off but decided to wait until morning to ask for scissors. My mother's voice in my mind said, *Don't make trouble.* I went to bed thinking about how I was going to make the ends of the cord match when I tied them in front. Cutting the wrong one or cutting off too much would be a disaster.

The following morning I awoke, immediately having the solution. I had solved the problem in my dream. The long side of the tie went the long way around the back side of my waist; then when I tied the ends, they were even. More importantly, I was thrilled to discover my ability to solve problems in my sleep. Wow! My Spiritual awareness was awakening.

With each of these milestones in awareness, my excitement rushed from me with a need to share my new insights. Although my mother experienced intuitive dreams, she never put any value in her experiences or mine. Usually, she said, "Go take care of your sister" or "Would you hurry up and finish that?" My mother's response was the same when I reported an unusual experience at the age of twelve.

Twice a day, afternoon and evening, I walked the mile to participate in the weeklong church revival services held each summer at the Baptist church we attended. During the mile walk back home, I pondered the words of the daily messages. During one particular week in July, the "altar call," which occurred at the end of every service, made me feel disturbed. It pressed many of my young friends into a fear- and guilt-releasing "walk the aisle" response. However, I was determined not to let intimidation push me into doing something that seemed contrived. I just wasn't going to do that! There had to be more to a conversion experience than walking the aisle. I wanted it, but it wasn't happening for me.

Dishwashing became a meditative action as well, a time for listening for insight from the Spirit world. I liked looking out the open window that hung over the double sink. The green pasture of red and white cows called to me, and birds seemed to carry the message of love.

On Thursday of the weeklong revival, while I was washing the lunch dishes and thinking about nothing, a brilliant light coming through the kitchen window suddenly overwhelmed me, flooding my body and heart, and spilling out through every pore of my skin. It was so bright that nothing else was visible. The light filled me with great joy and a clear knowing that the message of love must be shared, and then it was gone. I quickly dried my hands, ran outside to give my mother the message, and said, "We must tell the world about God's love. We can buy Bible storybooks for every child we know." (For some reason, I didn't tell her about the light. I think it was too much to explain. I only delivered the message.) Her response was the usual, "Have you lost your mind? Finish washing the dishes. Quit wasting time." I never told another of this experience until now.

The structure of our religion became the framework for my family's behavior, even when my parents disagreed with it. For instance, when we saw the preacher turn in the long driveway, we ran to change our shorts into jeans. We played cards and went to movies—but not on Sunday. I could dance if I was at the Methodist church, but I couldn't at the Baptist church. No one ever bothered to explain the discrepancy between our actions and beliefs. My interpretation became "When in Rome do as the Romans" and "It's okay if no one you know knows about it." However, belonging to a family with secrets bothered me. Secrets keep us from our real self. Where did your family's framework for behavior limit you?

By the time I was twenty, I had attended nursing school, joined the air force, married, and delivered two children eleven months apart. At thirty, I began teaching high school speech and drama. I was living my life in an active trance, a trance induced as a teenager to assist in my survival in the physical world. I was locked into living out cultural expectations. However, a Spiritual life doesn't stay asleep indefinitely. I began reawakening when I was thirty-two with my father's death. It took another seven years, which included another marriage and divorce, to wake me up and start me moving.

It was the reason for my being at Esalen Institute, sitting in the middle of the group, and asking the question, "Who am I apart from my parents, children, husbands, and careers?" My life no longer made sense. I felt as though I had died and left my body still living.

I sought psychotherapy, went back to graduate school in social work, and walked alone in the woods several miles a day for a year. My education in social work practice and my religious education didn't mesh. I valued both equally. What and who was right? How could they meet? The words from the Bible, learned as a teenager, rang in my ears as I walked. Words like "Once saved, always saved," "Salvation is an ongoing process," and Jesus' words, "...I am the way, the truth and the life. No man cometh unto the Father but by me" (John 14:6). How did this precept fit into the theories of mental health and character development? How could the secular world and the Spiritual world merge within me? A new life, a different *I*, began to occupy my body. My answers came over the next three years during my walking meditations and as a result of Bible study and my practice as a therapist leading a hospital recovery group for alcohol addiction.

As I walked, I learned. I began to experience what it means to be a conscientious living organism with the ability and responsibility to make choices with love. We arrive at human freedom by discovering and modifying aspects of self that don't serve us. It's in this response to freedom that a human being becomes authentic and fully alive. We are fully alive when our microcosm perfectly mirrors our macrocosm, when we are one with the universe, in harmony with all. When our Spiritual worlds, mental worlds, and physical worlds mirror each other, the result produces a more confident, unique way of being. We gain the ability to enjoy naturally unforgettable success and deep inner satisfaction as we accept and overcome the world through profound love. Most would agree that in this state, we best manifest creation's glory. We are real.

We all have in common this process of becoming. Change is unavoidable. We can be passive and victims of our own fate, or we can be responsible in creating the direction of our changing. I was willing to go the journey. However, I questioned, "The process of becoming—of becoming what?"

"The process of becoming as little children so we can enter the kingdom of heaven where love dwells. The process of selecting, through our power of free will, to live in the light of wholeness, God's love, or to live in darkness, separated from our own Divinity" was the answer I received. At that point, I began the task of directing my will toward Love.

Psychologist Rollo May in *Love and Will* points out that through expressing "I choose" and "I will," we create the expressions of our identity and our task is to unite our will with our heart in love through conscious development. "Conscious development"—ah, there is the challenge. In meeting this challenge, I soon discovered that it is in the repetitive use of our free will to choose to live in the light of wholeness, in Divine Love, that we become real and able to know who we truly are. For me to become real, I had to learn to love myself in a completely different way than the template, which my parents had given to me, had predestined.

The love demonstrated by the life of Jesus proved to be the best role model for loving myself. I knew from childhood that love could lift me up. We sang about it, but how was it done? I had to learn the process of choosing love for my internal self. I was determined to develop that skill. To do so, I needed to change my thinking process and match the diagram of the Spiritual world described in the Bible while honoring Sigmund Freud's concept of the human consciousness—id (unconscious, basic human needs), superego (preconscious or subconscious rules or beliefs), ego (balances id and superego).

First, I began to structure my thinking into four rooms in my mind, in accordance with the relationship between four major religious archetypes described in the Bible— Satan, Jesus, Divine Child and the Book of Life.

Second, because our thoughts manifest in physical form through our bodies, I began to monitor my body's response to the words of each archetype expressed through me.

Third, I monitored my actions for alignment with my thinking, creating internal peace through the realigning of my mental and physical worlds with my Spiritual one. I believed that by doing so, I would be doing my part in creating heaven in physical form on earth—in both my body and my actions.

Over a period of three years, I resolved my internal conflict between my newly acquired social work education and my childhood religious teachings by marrying psychology with Spiritual concepts that honor both. I call this process "A Sacred Trust: The Inner Child."

Beginning in 1990, I taught recovering addicts how to use this process as a step in their recovery. By 2005, it was included as part of a research-based mindfulness program called Grand Ideas from Within, which teachers and counselors teach in Louisiana public schools, grades six through twelve, and then in 2011 in Mississippi schools.

I have used this model for thirty years, and my life is remarkably satisfying—and my courage and confidence strong. Love is the choice I make for myself from moment to moment. Fear, anxiety, and negative judgments of others or myself no longer rule me. I encourage you too, to continue in this process.

Writing this book has been a continuation of this journey. I dreamed the title Healing Mind in 2003 while living in Louisiana, discovered the cover art in Alabama at an October Festival in 2011, and Norm Shealy wrote the foreword in 2014. When we are true to our authentic self, surprises happen every day. I celebrate you in your process of becoming your true authentic self and in loving the beautiful creation that you are.

Make the choice to live your life in alignment with your internal self, your real self. Explore your life's stories and discover how they are serving or armoring you against the world and in doing so, discover more love for yourself than you can even begin to imagine. How you think about yourself and the world changes everything.

Most of my hair has turned gray, and my joints are loose, but these factors don't really matter at all when we have lived our lives from that part of our self that is made real through love... as this selection by Margery Williams (1881–1944) from *The Velveteen Rabbit or How Toys Become Real* illustrates.

"Real isn't how you are made," said the Skin Horse. "It's a thing that happens to you. When a child loves you for a long, long time, not just to play with, but REALLY loves you, then you become Real."

"Does it hurt?" asked the Rabbit.

"Sometimes," said the Skin Horse, for he was always truthful. "When you are Real you don't mind being hurt."

"Does it happen all at once, like being wound up," he asked, "or bit by bit?"

"It doesn't happen all at once," said the Skin Horse. "You become. It takes a long time. That's why it doesn't often happen to people who break easily, or have sharp edges, or who have to be carefully kept. Generally, by the time you are Real, most of your hair has been loved off, and your eyes drop out, you get loose in the joints and very shabby. But these things don't really matter at all, because once you are Real you can't be ugly, except to people who don't understand."

STEP 1

BUILDING YOUR FOUNDATION OF SUPPORT

Healing Mind specifically describes a way of organizing your thinking and includes a series of practices intended to awaken you to your complete authentic self. In a sense, by practicing the techniques described herein, you will become your own therapist. Think of all the money you can save.

Our foundation of support is built on the premise that the dimensions of the Divine are the constituents of the mind and that the constituents of the mind manifest as the magnitude of the world. In other words, our imagination and perception fill our thoughts and our thoughts create the physical world.

The approach taken in this book is based on the premise that people must find their own way in life and accept responsibility if they hope to achieve maturity. It uses the technique of categorizing each thought based on the four Judeo-Christian archetypes: the Book of Life, Satan, Jesus, and the Divine Child.

We feel less threatened when we focus on the process of perceiving rather than attending to the content of what we perceive. Therefore, this process, rooted in the psychological theories of Jung, Gestalt, and psychodrama, along with neurolinguistic programming and cognitive therapy, focuses on your how rather than the what and why of the process.

In addition, this technique is phenomenological in that it centers on our perception of reality, it is existential in that it approaches the past and future in the here and now, and it is experiential in that we can come to grips with what we are thinking, feeling, and doing as we interact with our environment. Our goal is to stand on our own feet and give our own free response to the call of each moment. It is through this creative process that we learn ways to do the following:

- Take responsibility for, rather than project onto others, our own internal experiences.
- Become aware of our own needs and develop skills to satisfy them without violating others.
- Become sensitive to our surroundings while, at the same time, protecting ourselves from potentially destructive situations.
- Take responsibility for our personal actions and their consequences.
- Feel comfortable with the awareness of our own fantasy life and its expression.

According to George Weinberg, author of *The Heart of Psychotherapy*, a good therapist is born with certain traits of humanness that motivate him or her to acquire additional traits similar to those we will be using in this process. What Weinberg calls "basic humanness" includes an ability to (1) admit errors, (2) tolerate frustration, (3) and refuse to judge by appearances, age, or social class. A totality of these traits, when brought to a therapeutic setting, results in an interaction of growth primarily for the client and secondarily for the therapist. You will be doing this with parts of yourself.

Weinberg profiles a therapist by saying that there must first be an ability to feel and a readiness to respond. The client, on the other hand, usually is lacking in one of these two areas—the ability to feel or respond. Which is the weaker of the two for you—recognizing your physical sensations or your emotional sensations? Are you also, in turn lacking in your ability to respond to your body or your emotions once they are recognized? A *yes* or *not sure* answer means you have been settling for less than your life's full potential. The essence of most people's lives as they settle for less is exemplified through the lines delivered by the twenty three year old character, Eugene from the award winning play *Broadway Bound* by Neil Simon's *(1986)*.

> "I'll be honest about one thing. Dancing with my mother was very scary. I was doing what my father should have been doing with her but wasn't. And holding her like that and seeing her smile was too intimate for me to enjoy. Intimacy is a complex thing: you have to be careful who you share it with ... but without it, life was just breakfast, lunch and dinner, and a good night's sleep. Most people would settle for that. Most people do ... I was determined not to be most people."

The process described in the following pages, which you're about to undertake, uses Weinberg's characteristics of a good therapist as aspects of your mature adult personality. Playing the role of the therapist, you will mentor and nurture the Wounded Child part of yourself, the client. In the process, you're both the therapist and the client. As you develop, you will become aware of the "between realm"—not only between you and another person but also between two parts of yourself. Dr. Irvin D. Yalom, an emeritus professor of psychiatry at Stanford University, a practicing psychiatrist, and an author of numerous books, including *Theory and Practice of Group Psychotherapy*, has stressed throughout his years of practice that the relationship is what heals—the positive unconditional regard, nonjudgmental acceptance, authentic engagement, and empathic understanding.

Empathic understanding is the ability to know intuitively what is going on with another person. It requires the skill of taking down our personal boundaries and blending our energy with that of the other person or with another part of ourselves. This act also requires some of the remaining traits Weinberg describes as common to therapists, including the following:

- intelligence to judge the appropriateness of a given situation
- courage to let go of one's own ego boundaries without losing oneself
- flexibility to meet someone with love when he or she is ready and open
- insistent egalitarianism to enable unity of equals, creating a sense of family between another person and our self

The uncensored openness of being an insistent egalitarian is possible only when the preceding traits are present. Weinberg implies, between the lines of his writings, a felt presence of Spirituality, yet he doesn't specifically mention this as a profile trait. Personally, I experience it as the most important trait to facilitate the exchange of life between two people. This allows both sympathy and empathy to emerge in the "between realm" of the therapist and the client. Some call this sense of Spirituality a Spiritual or Divine Presence, openness to a Higher Power or God. Spirituality needs credit not only as a profile component but also as a motivating factor in the therapeutic setting. This is much like the man from an isolated country when first visiting America. When told about Jesus and what he could do in one's life, the man replied, "Oh I know him; I just never knew his name."

Schools of Thought on How People Change

There are three schools of thought on how people can change: (1) the psychoanalytical school, (2) the interpersonal school, and (3) the action therapies school. The psychoanalytical school of thought, such as Sigmund Freud, proposes that the personality congeals in early childhood. Sets of attitudes, feelings, and impulses, all of which are primarily unconscious, become frozen in personality. Over a lifetime, these forces evolve to dictate a person's behavior. Therefore, our beliefs or what we do, are merely a symptoms of who we are underneath, so changing our behavior is pointless. The interpersonal school of thought, as people like Karen Horney and Erich Fromm represent, takes the position that the individual's own actions as a child and afterward influence the formation of his or her personality. An individual is more than a passive being: one's actions influence others, whose reactions influence individual personality development at every stage. Everyday choice affects characteristic feelings and attitudes. The way a person treats others does, in fact, affect him or her indirectly.

The action therapies school, as Gestalt and psychodrama therapist such as Fritz Pearls, Joseph Zinker, and J. L. Moreno, MD, represent, helps the individual heal himself or herself by making changes in his or her personality traits. Action therapists believe people unknowingly keep themselves the same. Every choice reinforces underlying feelings, attitudes, and beliefs, creating a view of life that motivates the next choice. An action therapist's aim is to uncover generalities, traits within the personality, and to help people grow to a place of arriving at their own best answers. (Yes, you can learn how to do this for yourself.)

Any excessive actions, such as cigarette smoking, talking, and television watching, serve as an interruption of silence—an avoidance of our emotional condition in the moment, a way to keep ourselves unknown. The incorporated exercises intend to increase focused concentration. Silence, when joined with focused concentration, has the effect of building up the intensity of any emotional feeling to the point that it will become consciously known ... Really. Try it.

Action therapists see in a personality trait three components of the person—perception, emotion, and subsequent behavior. Joseph Zinker, author of *The Creative Process of Gestalt Therapy*, added a fourth component—expression. Perception, emotion, and behavior exist together;

a change in one changes the other. To complete the energy cycle inherent in all living things, one must perceive, feel, move, and express on one's own behalf.

Change manifests through our taking responsibility for our own thinking, feeling, doing, and expressing. The self-healing process you're about to learn follows the action therapist school of thought. It is through self-awareness that we gain self-understanding and through knowledge that we can know ourselves and choose to change.

Deprivation

How are you depriving yourself? We cannot reach our full potential when significant aspects of ourselves are deprived. Identifying and developing any areas that are lacking become the underlying goal of therapeutic sessions. Which of the following do you think are real deprivations for you?

- an inability to enjoy each moment
- an indifference to caring statements
- interpreting the actions of others
- focusing on judging self and others
- acting from fear based on past experiences
- worry, loneliness, or separateness
- high incidents of conflict
- making things happen rather than allowing them

You will want to keep these in mind as we work through this process. They will be your reference points for determining when and if you need more work.

An ability to be consciously aware of our feelings and act on our own behalf is inherent in the following Gestalt Therapy Energy Cycle (figure 1) for awareness and growth. It is our foundation map. Every movement, sentence, tone of voice— our sanity follows this map when we are real. If not, then we experience deprivation. The first step of the Gestalt Therapy Energy Cycle begins with grounding in the present as described in the following exercise.

• **Center Ground, the Present**

Do this exercise with your eyes closed while sitting in a straight-back chair or with eyes open while sitting or standing in public. Practice this when standing in line at a checkout counter or waiting in traffic until it becomes your second nature. Repeat this process internally anytime and anywhere.

Exercise 1: Gathering of Attention or Energy Focus within the Self

Suggestion: Record yourself while you slowly read the following script aloud and then listen to your recording.

Purpose: To allow for alertness, relaxation, and sensitivity to your inner world by placing your concentration on the center of your body at your waistline

Step 1: Loosen your clothes, place your feet flat on the floor, uncross your arms, and close your eyes. Take a few deep breaths, breathing in through your nose and out through your mouth.

Step 2: Imagine that the energy at the center of the earth is moving toward the surface of the planet. Through all the layers, it continues to move. It can go through the crust, the asphalt, the cement, the floor, and right through the carpet, through your shoes, and into your feet.

Step 3: Let the energy enter your legs. Feel it move up and go around your knees, up your thighs, and up to the base of your spine. When it reaches your spine, send it straight back down to the center of the earth—right through your spine, as if the energy were an extension of your spinal column, a tail. Your energy keeps moving in a complete circle from the center of the earth up into your legs, around to the base of your spine, and then straight back down to the center of the earth. When you're ready, open your eyes.

Gestalt Therapy Energy Cycle
Figure 1: Gestalt Diagram

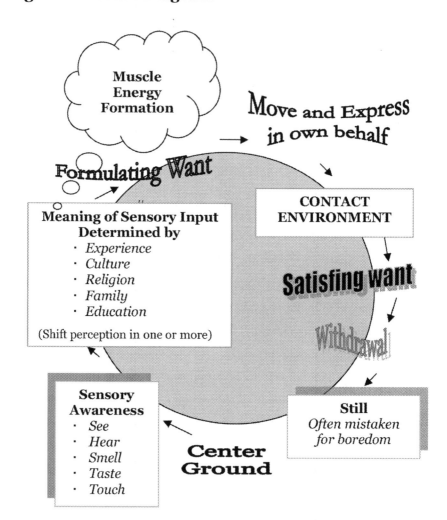

Muscle
Energy
Formation

Move and Express
in own behalf

Formulating Want

**Meaning of Sensory Input
Determined by**
· *Experience*
· *Culture*
· *Religion*
· *Family*
· *Education*

(Shift perception in one or more)

**CONTACT
ENVIRONMENT**

Satisfing want

Withdrawal

**Sensory
Awareness**
· *See*
· *Hear*
· *Smell*
· *Taste*
· *Touch*

**Center
Ground**

Still
*Often mistaken
for boredom*

• **Sensory Awareness**

The second step is to notice our sensory input. We must know what we feel (sensory awareness) to answer the question "Who am I?" While this may seem simplistic, throughout this process we will categorize all emotions into one of the following four feelings: glad, mad, sad, and afraid. In a pain-resulting situation, we are first afraid, then sad, followed by mad (anger). These three feelings hang together. To heal a painful memory, we travel back through these experienced feelings in reverse order, first encountering anger, then grief, and finally fear to arrive at glad (peace, joy). Glad is the payoff when the other three are resolved.

As babies, we see the world as it is. As we mature, we learn to see the world through others' belief systems. Our natural clarity dims. "Looking to see" rather than "seeing" becomes a way to avoid reality, a way not to "see" who we really are or what we truly need. Reclaiming our natural sight necessitates taking down those veils of illusion and in the moment seeing the world clearly as it is.

Our ability to distinguish between what is concrete and what is imagined in an innate form is what keeps us sane. To the extent that we are unable to distinguish, through any one of the five senses, the difference between what is present and what is inferred is the degree of our neurotic pain or dysfunction.

Our sensory capacities—vision, hearing, taste, touch, and smell—orient us toward our relationship with our environment, our outer world. Our five senses ground us in our environment and determine our relationship to it. We base our inner world and sense of reality on our degree of contact with our ground, our awareness through all our senses of what is present in the "now," not what we imagine to be present. We must learn to use our senses as receptors for personal clarity to distinguish between what we hear, feel, and see—what is imagined, what is labeled, and what is the Self.

Without clear inner physical sensations, we lose touch with the concept of who we are and what we need. Itching skin, muscular tension and movement, feelings and emotions, discomfort and well-being are all inner-world experiences. Our inner-world capacities include the following:

- proprioception: sense of location of body parts
- kinesthesia: sense of movement
- visceral sensation: fullness or emptiness of digestive organ and heartbeat
- pressure, pain, or pleasure
- sensation of thought and visual images

Once, I was browsing in a gift shop when the continuous playing of music in the background came into my foreground. The sound persisted in getting my attention. I thought I'd heard that music somewhere else, but I couldn't place where. Distracted now from my need to see what was in the store, I moved to where the music CD was on display for sale, and I purchased it. I played it over and over during my trip back home. Where had I heard that music before? The minute I arrived home, I realized I already owned the CD.

It is obvious which of my five senses is in the background—my auditory memory. I record first in my visual memory; then the sensations that go with what I see become part of my feeling memory, and finally any sounds I hear are in my audio memory. This is my mental strategy for committing information to memory. To retrieve any information from memory, I must go through the same strategy I used to store it. At the previously mentioned shop, I started with the last step in my strategy, the sound of the music, to try to recall where I had heard it in the past. I became lost in my mind. After arriving home and seeing where I usually listen to music, I remembered. When my lack of auditory awareness began to cost me money, I paid attention.

Both sounds and pictures can occur out of our awareness. However, with conscious effort we can bring them into our awareness and control. We can turn up the volume and listen. When we do this, we shift our perception.

• **Meaning of Sensory Input**

We think in words with rhythm, tempo, volume, and pitch. Consciously changing any of these produces a change in our internal experience. We think in pictures—moving or still, black and white or color. We can be in these pictures or observing them. The picture can appear close up or far away. All these choices are ours to make. A change in any of these components completely changes our internal experience and subsequently our perception of reality in the moment and as we remember it. Pay attention to your mental process. If you have PTSD (post-traumatic stress disorder), try making all the changes and see which ones cause the memory to lose its emotional power.

We determine the meaning of sensory input through interpretation; we hear, see, feel, taste, and assign meaning to all. To change, we must change our interpretation, our perceived dynamics, in one or more of the following areas:

- experience
- culture
- religion
- family
- education

Look at each of these five areas again. With each one imagine yourself making a change that could move your life forward. Which is the most difficult for you to imagine changing?

• Formulating a Want

Once we assign meaning to sensory input, our minds formulate a need, a want, from an array of possibilities— danger, hunger, fatigue, opportunity, or discomfort. Whatever surfaces to the top of our awareness begins a process of moving the necessary energy to our needed muscles for sufficient movement to satisfy the need. Hysterical behavior is a leak of energy at this point in the Gestalt Therapy Energy cycle (figure 1). Muscular energy is lost before it can intensify enough to produce the action for satisfying the need. Hand-wringing, screaming, excessive talking, and pacing are examples of ways people lose their drive to move on their own behalf.

Imagine that you're reading a book you really enjoy. A rumble begins in your stomach (sensory awareness). You notice the time: too early for dinner. You continue reading;

there's more rumbling. Hunger (meaning of sensory awareness) intensifies. Your mind begins to formulate a mental image of an apple (formulating a want), which overrides your want to continue reading. Energy builds as excitement in your muscles to move.

Excitement is our energy that focuses us toward the object of our need. When we are in doubt of what our need is, we may hold our breath and experience our unfocused excitement as anxiety. We are afraid of the consequences of being who are meant to be in the moment. In doing this we become dysfunctional at getting our needs met. We are deprived. Explaining, imagining, planning, interpreting, guessing, thinking, and comparing are inner-world activities, not present-moment activities. Thinking beyond the present and of an on-going experience is also mental activity that falls into this category of "not in the moment." Remembering the past and anticipating the future keep us out of present contact with our environment "out of the moment."

- **Move and Express on Own Behalf**

Energy is building in your legs and arms. You remember the apple in the bowl on the table. Your muscle energy reaches a peak. You put down the book, get up, walk to the table, and reach for the apple (partial contact with the environment) only to discover it's fake. You stomp your foot, exclaiming, "Oh, darn!" You experience an energy leak, which necessitates a pause as your mind regroups to imagine the crisper drawer of the refrigerator containing real apples, and new energy surges to your legs. (Contact that satisfies the motivating need of hunger isn't yet met.) Emergent needs are met only through interaction with the environment. All healthy contact involves both sensory awareness and a sense of excitement, resulting in spontaneity.

- ## Contact with the Environment

Contact with the environment is a continuous process, not a final state of achievement. We make contact through our five senses by interacting with nature and other people without losing our sense of individuality. Prerequisites for good contact are having clear sensory awareness, knowing our need, having full energy to move, and possessing the ability to express ourselves on our own behalf. Gestalt therapists remind us that contact is a continuous process of moving toward the environment to reach satisfaction and withdrawing into stillness—repeated again and again.

Moving forward, opening the door and then the drawer, taking an apple, rubbing it on your sleeve, taking a bite, chewing completely, swallowing—all these actions are necessary to have the apple contact your stomach with the intent to satisfy your hunger. Satisfaction causes hunger to drop into the background, and the need to continue reading rises to the foreground, moving you back to reading your book.

- ## Satisfaction of Want or Need

Where, when, and how in your body do you feel satisfaction? Satisfaction is worth savoring. Heighten your awareness of your sense of satisfaction. Look for satisfaction when eating or at the end of good sex, when you hear the words "I love you." We must remain aware of the sensation of satisfaction in our bodies; this is similar to what happens when we watch an awesome sunset fade into night. When we move our attention away from our sense of satisfaction toward the dawning of a new want too soon, we lose our ground, our body awareness (in other words, borderline personality disorder). Locate the sensation of satisfaction in your body, be with it in silence, and remain still, aware as the sensation withdraws.

• **Withdrawal**

To complete the contacting process, we withdraw to assimilate what we received and quietly remain, waiting for the moment of new simulation through our five senses (Figure 1: Gestalt Therapy Energy Cycle).

• **Stillness**

Stillness, often mistaken for boredom, follows the fading of the satisfaction sensation. Those uncomfortable with silence, such as during unresolved grief, intentionally avoid the stillness that follows satisfaction. When we embrace the stillness, we eventually return to new sensory awareness, where we can again begin the creative process of resolving our boredom, grief, or any other need coming into the foreground.

A Failed Gestalt: Stuck in Deprivation

To be able to feel, express, and act is the basic process of psychological growth in any individual. It is through this process that we can begin to reclaim our ability to self-nurture rather than to project our nurturing self onto others. A failed gestalt is the interruption of our energy flow at any point in the Gestalt Therapy energy cycle. A delay in the initial steps of walking or a hesitation in initiating a sentence is an example of a block at the point of Energy Formation, the beginning of movement in the Gestalt Therapy Energy Cycle (figure 1). Wherever the interruption occurs, whether at the beginning, middle, or end of the cycle, it will continue to be an interruption in the same way repeating it's self in everything we do, creating layers of deprivation.

We consistently interrupt our gestalt process in every action, as exemplified in the motion of the tennis serve or golf swing. Richard Strozzi Heckler describes in detail this point of interruption in the gestalt process in his book *The Anatomy of Change* (1984). Our pattern of being with interruptions or not, shows up in every move we make as well as in the way we relate to others. Is your process faulty or efficient?

When we are stuck in our gestalt process at the point of stimulation, we hold our breath and become tense. If our block is at the point of our Energy Formation, we refuse to feel an emotion and then claim we don't know what we want. When blocked at the Satisfaction stage, we can get some of what we want but not enough. Finally, when we block at the point of Withdrawal, we refuse to feel satisfaction.

The defense mechanisms, our armor acquired early in our lives keep us from completing the Gestalt Therapy Energy Cycle in any given moment. According to Gestalt therapy theorists, we have seven ways or styles of keeping energy pent up so we can pretend to remain the same. These ego defenses keep us from being authentic. We can deflect, desensitize, introject, project, proflect, retroflect, or become confluent. We choose one or more of these defenses when we make choices concerning all things experienced both internally and externally.

Desensitization is the restriction of body sensations from our awareness, which is a good way to manage pain but not so good for being present to our social and emotional needs.

Introjections and projections are defenses of our minds and thought processes. They occur at the point of sensory meaning on the Gestalt Therapy Energy cycle (figure 2). We "introject" when we fail to evaluate rationally and incorporate unconsciously new information from the world around us. It is the process of believing what others say about us without validating the information against reality. We use this one positively to cram for exams. When we passively incorporate what the environment provides, it remains the unassimilated other and not a part of who we really are. We call people like this "gullible." They swallow others' beliefs and standards without assimilating them congruently into their personality. We aren't what others have made up about us (projections of themselves). We are much more.

Figure 2: Defense Mechanisms That Interrupt the Gestalt Process

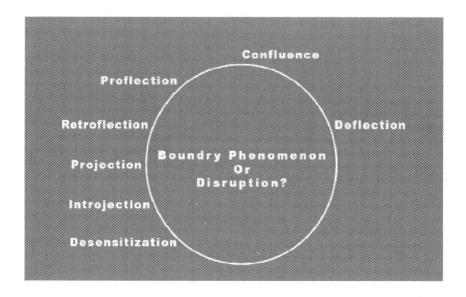

When you were a child, did anyone say things to you that are similar to the following? "Oh, you're such a bother." "You can't do anything right." "You're so lazy." Did you believe him or her? If so, you introjected the other person's projection. What someone said about you really describes him or her. He or she isn't really seeing you. Oh! You think there might be a little truth in what the person said. Well, maybe there is, but you'll never know until you ask yourself, "How am I bothersome or lazy?" Then ask, "When am I ...?" and "Where am I like that?"

These same questions can help us discover whose rules we are living. Any statement that contains a "should" is a swallowed rule that belongs to someone else, an introjection. When we chew the rule before swallowing it, we discover whether it is truly our value. "I should visit my mother" becomes

"I want to visit my mother" or "I don't want to visit her. I want to call instead." "What is my need?" is also a useful question in this process of discovering who we are.

The question that leads to nowhere is "Why?" It's a trap. The answer beginning with the word *because* is always a never-ending list of other reasons. Avoid asking and answering the question "Why?" Recall those times when one of your parents said, "Why did you do that?" and you tried to find the right "because." Usually, there was no correct answer, even though you anxiously tried to satisfy your parents' questioning. Most answers you gave didn't get you off the hook. You believed the reason was that you didn't pick the right "because." You had no way of knowing then that the answer to the question "Why?" is always an infinite "because," making it a pointless process.

People who use projections as a defense mechanism, as we all do from time to time, have difficulty in the moment telling the difference between their inside world and the inside world of the other person. Projections are disowned attributes of ourselves—attitudes, ideas, feelings—we assign to others as a defense against anxiety. They show up in our statements of blame, guilt, or responsibility. Statements that start with "You're ..." are usually our projections. They tell us more about ourselves than about the person targeted to receive the projection. Children and pets are usual recipients of our projecting more desirable traits. For example: "My dog knows just what I'm thinking. He is the smartest, kindest understanding dog I've ever seen." "My cat is just like me. We both like quiet afternoon naps."

Swallowed projections of others become our own *introjections* that erode our self-esteem, as do the projections of our positive characteristics onto others. "I wish I could be as kind as she is" is a projection of your own ability to be kind. If you can see a character trait in someone, whether judged good or bad, then that same trait also belongs to you. Being in love is a projection of your most lovable self onto another and loving you in him or her. That's why when you really get to know the other person, he or she isn't quite as wonderful as you first thought, because *you're* the wonderful person.

Owning the projection we placed onto someone else is done by adding "and so am I" at the end of the "you" statement or thought. "You're so kind, and so am I." "You're so thoughtless, and so am I." This step will defuse the critical "you statements" of an argument every time. At first, you will want to say, "No, I am not like that." However, continuing in this process will heighten your awareness of those miniscule moments when "so am I" is true. This creates an opportunity for self-acceptance.

Retroflection, the fourth defense mechanism, occurs at the point of Move and Express on the Gestalt Therapy Energy Cycle and is harder to recognize unless it is extreme, as in self-mutilation. We retroflect when we do to ourselves what we would like to do to others or what we would like someone to do to us. Our energy builds up in our muscles to reach out to get or remove something from our environment we need to sustain our existence. Before our energy can contact the environment, we redirect it, substituting ourselves for the object of our own actions. We slap our faces instead of his or hers and hit our heads as if to knock some sense into them with a "Duh!" when we really want to knock sense into his or her head. We hug other people when the truth is, we want them to hug us.

The release of our body tension ready for action is only partially satisfied when we retroflect. The need that produced the buildup of muscular energy is never really met, because the object is the source of the need. Retroflecting, turning our energy back onto ourselves, interrupts the cycle that leads to true satisfaction. We continue this repetitive cycle of dysfunction and dissatisfaction until we increase our awareness with the questions "What am I doing? When am I doing it? How am I doing this?" To discover even more about yourself, ask the question "What is my need to be hugging this person, hitting my head, and so on?"

Proflection, the fifth defense mechanism is the process of self-dishonesty, of self-hiding, of manipulation. We use this to change the mental state of another through specific changes to ourselves, which we create. Normally our body sensations, plus the meaning we assign to them, direct us to move to fulfill our own perceived need. However, when we want to change others our actions depend on what we *think* the other person needs from us. It is always bidirectional since it requires feedback.

For example, when interviewing for a job, we share selected circumstantial information about ourselves with someone that creates in him or her an image we want him or her to have of us. How many times have you acted like you were enjoying an event so as not to hurt the feelings of the person with you or so he or she would believe you both liked the same things and would invite you again?

The sixth mechanism, confluence, occurs further around the Gestalt Therapy Energy cycle somewhere between Express and Contact. When we give over our creative energy to others, we are in confluence. People with weak personal boundaries and undefined selves, and those afraid of their own aggression prefer this defense mechanism to all the others. When we passively go along, we are in confluence. Confluence occurs when someone says to you, "I want to eat Italian food tonight at Portobello's. Do you want to go?" You reply, "If you want me to." Your vocal energy drops at the end of the statement because you really aren't in an Italian-food mood, but you want to have dinner with the other person. You give your energy away and fail to express your truth. Usually this response indicates that you are afraid of conflict or afraid of expressing your real opinion.

Maybe you sell yourself out because you think what you want isn't worth your standing up for it. If you really wanted to eat Italian food at Portobello's and be with the other person, your vocal energy would be strong at the end of the statement, expressing your spontaneity. There wouldn't be the implied "I guess" at the end as it is in the first response.

Another defense mechanism, deflection, is the process of distracting ourselves so we can avoid contact with our environment. The statements women use the most when others compliment them on what they are wearing are "Oh, I got this on sale," "This old thing?", or "I didn't have anything else to wear." Evidence of deflecting can show up in the overuse of humor, abstract generalizations, and questions rather than "I statements." We deflect when we fail to take in kind words, when we pass them off with, "Oh, they were just being nice." (Watch out for that *just* word. It suppresses your energy somewhere in your body.)

Avoiding contact through deflection is one of the ways we deny our spontaneity; we starve our Souls of positive Spirituality. Even conveying a superior attitude can be a means of deflecting. One example is when someone gives you a present as an act of gratitude; rather than accepting it and feeling the gratitude freely given in the expression of a gift, you say, "Oh no. I can't take it" or "You take it" and think, *I will never use this.* You're displaying a future-minded thought rather than a present-moment, in-the-now experience of acceptance.

Notice how you respond the next time you receive a complimented. As you learn to stop deflecting, ask that the person repeat positive statements. Allow yourself to feel what it is like to receive positive energy from someone. (Personally, I can handle only three consecutive positive statements, and then I have to ask for a pause before I can receive more.) Deflection might occur when you're in a group receiving positive regard from everyone or in a receiving line. If these positive comments were money, you would want them all. Decide to receive all the emotional and Spiritual awards given to you.

Shifting Perception: Mind Bridge

Stopping the interruptions in our Gestalt Therapy Energy Cycle and undoing our deprivations are impossible without shifting our perspective and, in turn, our perception. We use our ability to shift perception to distinguish our outer experiences from our internal ones, to identify objects from people and ourselves from others. Perception includes mental images of the environment received through our five senses and given meaning based on our previous experiences.

Biologist Bruce H. Lipton, PhD, has written a fascinating and inspiring book, *The Biology of Belief.* In it he explains that our behavior can be "controlled by invisible forces, including thought, as well as physical molecules like penicillin." He goes on to explain that our thoughts affect the cells of our bodies by creating an "above the gene (epigenetic) environment." This thought-created environment then signals our genes to select, modify, and regulate our gene activity. In other words, our perceptions are thoughts that motivate our responses to life all the way down to a single cell.

Since our thoughts can influence our body's chemistry, the environment in which cells live (Lipton), it stands to reason that perfecting our thinking to create a more supportive and loving epigenetic environment would be another step toward conscientious living (Shealy), enhancing our ability to live longer, be healthier, and have more satisfying lives.

A better inner life creates a better outer one, and shifting our perception changes aspects of our inner lives. When our perceptions are fixed, our actions are fixed as well. They create our habits. Our habits affect our physical, emotional, and Spiritual health, and by not taking conscious responsibility for this process, we give up our free will. A habit doesn't change without a change in perception.

Perception involves the whole brain. Western style of learning primarily uses the left brain. Learning to ride a bike, to read and write, and to do math (as well as speaking, logical thinking, and rational analytical thinking) are examples of left-brain activities. Lawyers, accountants, and engineers are left-brain professions. Most Americans are left-brain dominant. Eastern styles of learning use the right brain. Activities of the right brain consist of nonverbal and visual tasks, such as actually riding a bike, painting, dancing, and composing. Our intuition is a right brain activity.

Learning to monitor your thoughts and actually practice this process every day requires a move from the left side of your brain to the right side. Stopping critical dialogue takes a shift from your left brain to your right brain as well. Moving from the left brain to the right brain is an "aha" experience. Action therapy provides many opportunities for an "aha" experience. Use your whole brain. Those who place a series of actions into a single word, such as *love, sin,* or *lazy,* must move from the right brain to the left and itemize actions that carry the meaning of expressions of love or wrongdoing.

Figure 3: Balancing Your Brain

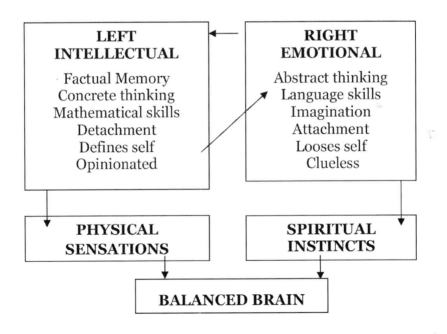

The following outline, based on the communication theory of neurolinguistic programming (NLP), illustrates how our perceptions, along with our senses, have meaning through language patterns.

Our Language Processing Model

I.   External events: sensory input—auditory, visual, kinesthetic, taste (gustatory), smell (olfactory) (A, V, K, G, O)

First, we receive an external event from our environment through our five senses and select one sense as foreground. Our internal filters created from previous perceptional experiences, acquired through our family, culture, religion, and education, encode this input and determine which information to delete or distort for generalizing. We delete sensory awareness when we want to motivate ourselves to finish a project. Obsessive-compulsive behavior is a repetition of this process.

II.   Internal processing filters: Encode input to determine how information is deleted or distorted for generalizations.

    A. Meta programs
       1. Internal process
       2. Internal state

    B. Attitudes
    C. Values and beliefs
    D. Memories
       1. Representation of time
       2. Conscious and unconscious decisions

Our generalizations create meta programs, which determine our internal process and our internal state; we form our attitudes, values, and beliefs; and we store memories. Our memories become representations of both time and conscious (and unconscious) decisions. By this point, nothing we remember is exactly as it occurred in the moment it happened, because of the many details left behind. This process determines 95 percent of our thinking, of which we are unaware. Conversely, if we delete too much from our awareness, we become mentally unable to function in our environment. Those with autism or Asperger's syndrome become overwhelmed with sensory input and are unable to delete input and create the needed meta programs for recognizing subtle differences in speech tone, pitch, and accent that give meaning to others' speech. Deleting sensory awareness is a basic universal modeling process.

III.   Universal modeling process

    A. Deleting sensory awareness: placing into background one or more sensory inputs (V, A, K, O, G)
    B. Distorting sensory awareness: misrepresenting reality to aid in motivation

IV.   Decoding sensory input—generalizing
V.   Internal representation

    A. Is used to create an internal representation for memory.
    B. The mind holds only seven items (plus or minus two) of information.

VI.   Language representation: Output through sentence structure

Next, as seen in the outline, we create an internal representation for the selected foreground sensory input—pictures, sounds, smells, sensations, tastes—through words. Quickly, we shrink all that sensory input into seven, plus or minus two bits of information into our language representations. We may have difficulty finding the words to adequately express our internal representation and add movement, art, or music to our words. People with dyslexia have difficulties at this communication point. Representation errors are errors in sentence structure that lead to miscommunication, which interferes with our getting our needs met—a failure in our gestalt process.

VII. Representation errors in sentence structure leading to miscommunication

    A. Lost performative
    B. Unspecified verb
    C. Universal qualifier
    D. Cause or effect
    E. Unspecified referral index
    F. Nominalization
    G. Mind reading
    H. Operator of necessity or possibility

(If you are searching the Internet for a more detailed explanation of each type of representation error, follow each with the letters *NLP*.)

In the seventies, a friend reported that his very young son had picked up a Christmas catalog; the cover displayed a child's naked backside (there are laws against this now). His son began to cry and said, "Why did someone take a picture of me without my clothes?" At the time we thought his response was cute and funny. However, in reality, he was unable to distinguish the child on the cover from himself. He may reach adulthood, recall this childhood memory, and think it really happened to him, believing that he was on public display for his parents' entertainment or gain. He may even make an appointment with a therapist to change his perception of this memory and concurrently his belief of exploitation.

Another child could see the picture and feel special to have his or her picture on the catalog. He or she then becomes the adult who feels entitled in life. Even at age three, we have already acquired our parents' perceptions, right or wrong, and have embraced beliefs and behaviors regarding nakedness. These handed-down perceptions and beliefs determine the difference in what each child perceives.

It is common for people to come into therapy, unaware that they are confusing what they see with what they imagine they see. For example, you see the furrowed brow of someone's face and imagine, based on your experiences, that the person is unhappy, maybe angry. Someone else with a different life experience can imagine the frowning individual to be in pain. All you really see in the moment is the frown. Everything else is made up from past perceptions or misperceptions, as we remember experiencing them. Blocks in perception, like ripples from a stone cast into water, radiate through all aspects of our lives.

A perception difficulty may begin at a young age with a problem in focusing the eye muscles, speculated to be the result of not enough crawling, and often requires an occupational therapist's intervention. After a certain point of maturation, if children are unable to make perception shifts, they will confuse reality and fantasy when relating events. As children progress in age, we become less tolerant when they confuse fantasy and reality, especially when they are older than the age of nine, around the age when we can distinguish concrete from abstract thinking.

Our ability to shift perception between reality and fantasy becomes clearer with maturation. To make changes in our lives, we must be able and willing to change our perceptions about life in one or more of the five areas previously listed in the Gestalt Therapy Energy cycle under Meaning of Sensory Input.

- experience
- culture
- religion
- family
- education

My first real conscious crisis between perception and action came when I was thirty-two and contemplating a divorce. I grew up in a strong religious family that supported the religious belief of no divorce. My father's favorite saying was, "You made this bed. Now lie in it." I found it extremely difficult to leave my nice, hardworking, deacon-of-the-church husband we all loved. It would have been equally difficult, even if I'd had justifications such as, "He was an abuser, an addict, a womanizer." No excuse passed; divorce wasn't an option for members of my family. I was stuck with the bed I'd made. My conflict resonated with the cells in my body, threatening my health and manifesting as unhappiness. I lost weight and sleep trying to fulfill roles—the good daughter, good wife, good mother, good Christian.

My fear, which resided in the background of my awareness, moved into the foreground, revealing its source. I wasn't allowing my perception of religious beliefs and my family values to change. I had to be willing to experience in my imagination my images of shame and rejection from those I loved, from my church and family, before I could take any action. In reality it wasn't that my family would absolutely reject me; however, I had to be willing to confront those images and beliefs of rejection to move forward. I had to take the risk and be okay with my not following all the rules of religious dogma. I had to trust my decision as the best one for me and act on my own behalf. I shifted my awareness, changing my perception of what God wanted for me; a change occurred in my perception of certain religious beliefs, resulting in my being more open minded and compassionate toward others and myself. My self-confidence soared.

A perception shift most often results in leaving us with more options, more room for psychological growth to become stronger, fuller beings. So, what was the reason for my divorce? Some moments are beyond reason. However, my father's death the previous year had greatly influenced me—a story for another time.

Ideally, we want to be able to experience both our complete inner world as well as the totality of contact with the environment through our five senses, and have them congruent and balanced. For example, you are driving down the interstate and see (outer world) the car ahead make a quick lane change in front of you. You imagine (inner world) that the lane change is the move of a reckless driver (projection). You become aggravated (inner world) and begin to tailgate him (dysfunctional behavior—you're acting out your projection of the reckless driver). The driver in the car next to you sees (outer world) the same thing, imagines (inner world) there is some difficulty ahead, and slows down in response (inner and outer congruence). A third driver sees (outer world) the same thing, but what he or she sees quickly falls into the background and out of his or her awareness. This driver is lost in another world of a repeated argument he or she had with his or her boss. Nothing happens this time because of his or her disassociation from the present. This, however, is the making of an accident.

Look at the following image. Focus on the white space first, pulling it forward into the foreground with your eyes. What does it look like? Two faces or a chalice? Shift your perception, allowing the white to recede into the background as you focus on the black, which now comes out of the background and goes into the foreground. See the chalice.

Figure 4: Foreground or Background

This is a simple example of shifting perception. You cannot see both images at exactly the same time, and you will prefer one to the other for the foreground. Your eyes' preference for one versus the other will remain the same each time you look at any art object containing black against white or white against black. There is no right or wrong answer. It's simply white space shared with black, isn't it? It's whatever we choose it to be.

Rigidness is a slow death. Dare to see the world from another's point of view without judgment. Stay flexible to choose from the world's limitless possibilities.

When I first saw Birdie May, she was quiet, intense looking, and contained. As I watched her enter the room, I tried to imagine how her perception of reality created her body armor. She had paid attention to her hair and makeup. Her attire, though neat, feminine, and conservative, suggested possible economic struggle. In some way, she was holding back her grace and beauty in the subdued colors she'd selected.

On one occasion, she arrived late and quietly blended into the group circle, almost as though she felt some disgrace in being there with the others or as though she didn't belong. There was no attitude of superiority or entitlement but rather a sense of guilt for wanting to participate. Her eyes sometimes filled with tears in contradiction to her smile. Others' experiences seemed to easily move her, yet she shared very few of her own. She frightened easily and looked especially scared when she became the focal point of the group's attention.

As Joseph Zinker suggested in *The Creative Process of Gestalt Therapy*, I created a mental metaphoric image for Birdie May, as her name suggested. I envisioned a bird with characteristics matching those I observed in her body. *How was she like a bird?* I wondered. Had her mother announced something by naming her Birdie? *Was she a symbol of the arrival of spring like a robin and protected by law?* It was easy to imagine Birdie suddenly flying away. Maybe she'd been named Birdie May in hopes that she would fly away.

Just as a bird persistently pursues a worm, she tenaciously went after what she wanted. She was determined to make a change. I continued to work with the bird metaphor, keeping what was useful and letting go of what wasn't a fit.

By the third session, Birdie May was ready to try her wings. She had practiced the perception-shift exercises and decided to try something on her own, to be spontaneous. She expressed a desire to leave the group for a while and go outside.

The group addressed how she'd stopped herself from getting what she wanted, how she wasn't giving herself permission to act on her own behalf. In the process she discovered her internal mother's voice telling her she couldn't leave the group. As Birdie worked through the energy present in the moment, her perception shifted, and she gave herself permission to leave. (Surprisingly, the group remained undisturbed by her leaving or by her return twenty minutes later.)

As she returned, she carried a handful of white gardenias picked from a stranger's yard. Another risk. She held them tightly until the end of the session and then gave all but one to me. She had no way of knowing they were my favorite flower and that as I'd passed the neighbor's yard on the way to the group, I too had wished for a bouquet but hadn't acted spontaneously. I'd respected the owner's boundaries. Was it her intuition, her information gathered from the "realm between," that had prompted her to give me the flowers?

The next week Birdie May was ready to do the individual work in the group. She could identify and separate her adult intellectual thinking from her critical, nurturing, and child thinking. She found a voice and physical expression for each category as the process unfolded; and, in turn, one of these compartmentalized mental parts revealed new information. (Further explanation of this process, A Sacred Trust: The Inner Child, follows in later sections.)

Over time, Birdie's history revealed itself. As an illegitimate child, she had never known her real father. Abortion had been illegal at the time of her conception (protected by law). The inner-child part of her personality confirmed a felt sense of being loved and wanted. However, her ambivalence remained.

"I think I'm loved and wanted, but how can I be sure?" She doubted her perception of her life experiences.

Birdie May's mother had married when Birdie was two years old and had allowed Birdie to believe her stepfather was her real father until she was eight and her stepfather and mother divorced. Birdie May was then told the truth.

"He says he loves me, so why doesn't he treat me like his child?" was Birdie's unresolved question.

"Maybe I was fooled, and he didn't love me after all, like I was fooled about him being my real father."

Birdie held onto the belief that she couldn't trust her perceptions. She'd been fooled once. Maybe she was being fooled all the time. She also believed men were unavailable. These beliefs motivated her to marry a Spiritual leader, whom she later discovered to be an addict. This discovery, in turn, reinforced her internal belief statement. "See, things are never as they appear."

The group focus shifted to helping Birdie May sort a real worm from those she labeled as such. They humorously encouraged her to give up worms and go for birdseed—less work, more variety, and more nurturing.

As she worked with the dialogue between her mental constructs, Birdie's perception shifts began to take on clear, distinct boundaries. She could see both sides of a situation without getting lost in the middle. She used her free will to choose a perception that allowed her to grieve her losses and then perceive even more choices available to her. Birdie became more congruent in her appearance and responses. She was also more visible in other social groups. Birdie May, in teaching her inner Child to shift her perception, freed herself to become more of a woman, revealing her hidden strengths. Her masculine and feminine characteristics came into balance. Birdie's changes in perception changed how she processed her thinking in regard to her life experiences.

Our process is the reason for our failures and successes. Uncovering our personal process aids us in getting what we want. Even now as you read this passage, there is a holding of tension in your body somewhere. Notice it. Breathe and notice any physical discomfort you keep in the background. Allow yourself to make the needed adjustments. As you find your area of comfort, reflect on your process of becoming. How are you doing what you're doing? Did you change because I reminded you to pay attention to your body or because you became aware of your discomfort through your body? There is a difference. The latter is preferred.

Exercise 2: Refine Your Process of Thinking—Change Perspective to Shift Perception

The following are powerful phrases that can change your perspective. From one perspective, the person leaves you, and from the other perspective, you leave him or her. Hold a picture in your mind of an important person in your life and say each statement aloud. You may envision a different person for each statement. Notice what happens to the picture, to the tactile information and/or sound as you speak aloud one of these statements to someone you're imagining. In your mind's eye, see the person moving away from you or you moving away from him or her. Release the person from your imagination with the phrase "And this is my existence." Saying, "And, this is my existence" keeps you in the "now." You may wish to write about your experience when you're finished to anchor your new skills in shifting perspective. What did you discover about yourself? Did you also experience an accompanying shift in perception?

Five Powerful Phrases to Shift Perspective

(He or she leaves you.)

1. I release you, and this is my existence.
2. I accept you as you were/are, and this is my existence.
3. I thank you for my lessons of life, intended or not, and this is my existence.
4. I free you, and this is my existence.
5. I am a unique, separate individual, and this is my existence.

(You leave him or her.)

1. I leave you, and this is my existence.
2. I accept myself as I was/am, and this is my existence.
3. I accept myself for being a piece of your life lesson, and this is my existence.
4. I free myself, and this is my existence.
5. I am one with all, and this is my existence.

Figure 5: Shifts in Perception Boundaries

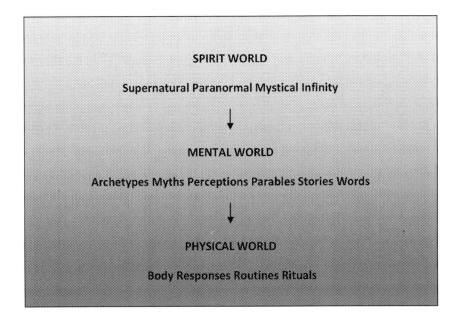

PART 2

SPIRITUAL MOTIVATION

Self-Actualizing, Self-Transcending

For there are three that bear record in heaven, the Father, the Word, and the Holy Ghost: and these three are one.

—1 John 5:7

Figure 6: Maslow's Hierarchy of Human Needs

(6) Self-transcendence—becoming more than the self, more than the body

  (5) Self-actualizing—become all of what one is capable of becoming

    (4) Self-esteem—feeling good about yourself, internal nurturing

      (3) Psychological and social needs— acceptance, belonging, love

        (2) Safety needs—security, stability

          (1) Physical needs—air, water, food, shelter, sex

SPIRITUAL WELLNESS

Spiritual wellness is the need that calls us into personal growth. It is the medium between therapist and client, in which both sympathy and empathy emerge (as explained in Step 1) and now between the Nurturer and Child part of you.

As living organisms, we are ever growing and changing as we move through Maslow's hierarchy of needs, needs that must be met to sustain growth. Maslow describes in his hierarchy of human needs the progressive movement from survival needs to self-actualization needs, and finally to the need for self–transcendence (added when he was sixty-eight). Our bodies carry the potential for self-knowledge, self-healing, love, and compassion. By reawakening the perceptive skills and acting on our own behalf, we allow the wisdom of the body to emerge. This guides us to create peace in our bodies where we live.

It is our human nature that calls us to meet the need to transcend—to transcend our aloneness and pain, and to feel a personal closeness to others, God, or nature and to the Spiritual aspects of life. When the first four levels of our needs go unmet through denial or abusive interference, the fifth-level need, self-actualizing, cannot emerge completely; consequently, neither can the sixth, self-transcendence. The quest for answers, more than an actual answer, indicates that we are on the path to transcendence.

As young children, we all at times experienced the pain of not getting our needs met at Maslow's levels one through four. When this happens repetitively, we experience deprivation within our self-esteem. In response, we create the five layers of the onion, which Gestalt theorists describe as the layers of neurosis. These layers limit us from achieving true transcendence. Layers named from the outer layer to the inner heart of the individual are the following: phony, phobic, impasse, implosive, and explosive. They keep us stuck in our internal process at level four, low self-esteem.

The phony layer is the layer of good manners—it is useful at times, dysfunctional at other times, and always the first layer to be laid aside on the way to revealing our true selves. Notice this the next time someone says, "Hello, how are you?" Feeling tired and frustrated, you respond, "Fine, thank you." There is nothing real happening in the exchange. Each individual is being phony. The one asking the question usually doesn't truly want to know how you are, and you don't want to tell him or her.

At the phobic layer of our metaphoric onion, we try to avoid the emotional pain of unmet needs created when we were children. We avoid being vulnerable. We don't want people to see that part of ourselves that was so unworthy of receiving what we needed. Our young minds perceive no other reason for a parent to deny our needs other than to think, *Something must be wrong with me.* We're afraid others will see this imagined defect and continue to deny our needs as well. We even create catastrophic fears of rejection when we simply imagine someone can really see us.

As we continue our journey inward, we find we are stuck in our own maturation at the third layer of dysfunction, the impasse. We've convinced ourselves that we don't have the inner resources to move beyond this stuck point without environmental support. At this point, our dysfunctional behavior manifests in our attempt to manipulate our environment into seeing, hearing, feeling, thinking, and deciding for us.

When we give up our connection to the environment by shutting out our five senses, we feel a sense of deadness. We think we're nothing. This circle of fear builds on itself. To escape and feel alive, we must fully experience our numbness, our deadness. I can hear you saying, "Now, how am I going to do that?" Keep in mind that all this fear of self-discovery is an illusion. Everyone else can already see what you cannot. I assure you this can be fun. You will be in full control; no one will see you. I will explain the process very simply in a later section.

Because we learned most of our behaviors before we were six years old, they are habitual, and habitual behaviors are stored in our subconscious where they run on autopilot. Only a small portion of our brains operates to make conscious choices. We have free will and can choose to travel to our subconscious mind by means of an altered state of consciousness. We can do this through numerous ways, such as self-hypnosis or meditation. In our altered state, we travel to the fourth layer, the implosive state, the path to the authentic self. Here we expose our defenses and begin to make contact with our genuine self at the fifth layer, where we explode with our own excitement, our released creative life energy. Each time we make this inward journey, we become more real to the world *and* to ourselves.

Finally, when we return from our unconscious mind to our conscious one, our energy withdraws and integrates what we've experienced. Once integrated, we savor our satisfaction and remain calm and still until our innate life's energy moves us to meet a new need, which might be one as simple as opening our eyes or standing up. We begin and complete the journey through the Gestalt Cycle again and again and again.

The majority of us live out our lives stuck in internal conflict, and our pain is inevitably reproduced in the world. Our unmet needs, when stuck at the impasse level of functioning, not only explain our destructive behaviors but also produce the motivation for our goal setting.

Businesses base their goals on things such as resources available from the environment, the capability of man or woman power within the company, and the desired economic return. With an eye toward the goal, employees are hired or fired, new products are added, and expansions are made. Whatever the action, it is in support of the goal. The future goal takes over the present moment. Goal setting, as we normally perceive it, supports internal misalignment in the moment by denying the self through performance. A rigidified goal takes on more energy at the expense of the individual, often manifesting as an obsessive-compulsive trait. To the degree that there is misalignment with the present moment, there is dysfunction—neurosis.

According to Weinberg, "What people strive for is nearly always within them, or else they can put it there." In other words, the achieved goals that satisfy the individual must be the size of the individual's talents, interest and resources. They must come from within. The goal is pliable when the inner world and external world are in alignment, when the microcosm perfectly mirrors the macrocosm.

What makes the difference between those who can make dreams come true and those who do not? An awareness of our body's sensations, our needs, and our abilities to move toward what we need in the moment becomes the bridge that connects the imagination and reality, the Spiritual to the physical, our real self. Your dreams can become your reality as you experience the meaning of contentment, pleasure, energy, and success. Crossing the chasm between our dreams and fantasies into the everyday world of our reality is an impossible task for some and a mere walk in the park for others.

Our innate resources, the way we use these resources, and the satisfaction or dissatisfaction we experience when doing so combine to project a satisfactory outcome. Clearly, a goal can give the present moment a focus point. However, no medication, hard work, or talk therapy is enough to bring about the healing of our Spirits lost in the misalignment of the moment. While goals enable us to lay some ground for self-actualization, they will not heal us Spiritually. What will help us is an understanding of our personal history and the forces that have shaped our lives.

To reach self-transcendence, we must alter a destructive inner way of living. To bring new life, we need some means of establishing and keeping alive the ongoing relationship with our inner Child, a concept popularized in the nineties and in truth is as old as the teachings of Christianity.

Monitoring our own minds becomes a moment-by-moment act of free will that begins the process of creating over time a Spirit-filled life. In other words, you're a saved Soul (another familiar Christian archetype) by manifesting as your internal process the characteristics of the archetypal Jesus.

The difficult part is in paying attention—staying awake and changing our dialogue in the moment. The choice is to wake up to what is going on in your mind or to sleep through this life, wasting your gift of free will, your freedom to choose. Take charge and create a practice that will give you the kind of life you deserve. It all begins inside you. You have nothing to lose. You always have the choice to return to the way you were or do nothing.

Harvard Medical School has systemically studied the benefits of mind/body interaction for more than twenty-five years. Their research shows that when someone engages in a repetitive sound, phrase, or prayer, he or she disregards intrusive thought. Specific physiological changes follow that help to reduce hypertension, palpations, insomnia, and chronic pain. Metabolism, heart rate, and breathing frequencies all decrease, and slower brain waves occur. These changes are exactly the opposite of those stress induces. Their research also established that people experience increased Spirituality because of eliciting this state of consciousness (an opening to the subconscious), regardless of whether they used a religious repetitive focus. The report affirms, "Spirituality was expressed by the study participants as an experience (close to the person) of the presence of a power/force as energy, of what was perceived as God." (Video, *Healing Words, Healing Practices*)

Crossing the Chasm

When we completely focus on our bodies, We are present with our self, in the zone. It is from this energetic state of presence that universal knowledge flows through us, and we communicate it to the world. Our Spirit self is in accord with our physical self through the bridge of the mind. It is from this state of presence that authentic contact occurs. You probably know people whose presence you enjoy. Take a moment and describe what it is about that person that provides you the opportunity to be joyful.

Figure 7: Present at the Crossroad of Time

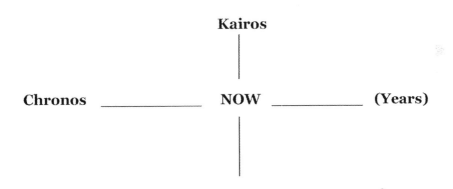

We are in a state of peace when we are at attention with, or focused on, our rushes of life energy, our excitement. Without presence, contact is one-dimensional. It's like talking about something you've read compared to talking about firsthand experience. When we make contact, the process of transmitting meaningful information through touches, emotions, nonverbal gestures, and energy fields, we are able to connect with the Spirits of living things and release our excitement, our joy, into the world.

Try looking at an object, such as a lamp or door; focus all your attention on the object. Notice your body sensation in relationship to an "it," a lifeless object—a door. Notice how often you treat another human being as an object. Now, focus all your attention on a present-living person. It can be a total stranger. See this person in this moment as your connection to all living things, a "thou," a Spiritual presence; this is the process of distinguishing a real person from a mannequin. We need to be able to do both to be fully alive.

We're able to choose presence when we know the sensational difference between an "it" and a "thou" (Martin Buber). We choose the feeling of an "it" when we want to be detached, emotionally unaffected by others. We choose the sensation of "thou" to be present, connected to others.

One of my significant memorable experiences of being in an "I and thou" encounter came about with a complete stranger. Unsure of the directions of my destination, I drove into a parking lot and stopped my car next to the passenger side of a van with the window rolled down. The man who was sitting there, seeing my car from his peripheral vision, turned in my direction and smiled. He looked intently into my eyes, being totally present, as I asked for directions.

There was a sense of peace about him. I felt as if I were in the presence of a great Spiritual leader. I asked my question, and I opened to receive information from him. At that moment, I felt his total life energy as a powerful giving force touching me. He gave me his presence, his total focus and concentration, his Spirit. I hadn't expected so much. I was overwhelmed but automatically responded in like kind. (I get tears now as I remember this awesome moment.)

A woman came out of the store and got into the car on the driver's side. Feeling the movement of the car as she entered, the man turned to her and spoke in sign language. He was deaf. The woman gave me the needed directions, and I was on my way, blessed by the "I/thou encounter," the real presence of another without his speaking a word.

Most people I encounter are too guarded, unavailable for this kind of intimate contact. On the other hand, children are much more open to present-moment contact, the moment when trust and love is shared and we both feel the physical sensation of each other's Spiritual essence. It is more than giving another our attention. It is touching their Spirit with our own. My oldest grandson first made this kind of conscious connection with me when he was eighteen months old. We call this "love." By age nine, after such a moment of contact he asked, "Now what, Grand Mama?" As an adult, he continues to seek moments with me for real presence.

There is nothing more than the present-moment encounter. We are human beings in a physical world *and* Spiritual beings in a physical body. We open to have Spiritual experiences and close to create boundaries suitable for meeting the demands of the world around us. Both the "I" and the "thou" are transformed by the relation between them.

Archetypes

Psychologist Carl Jung, knowing all along that there is an archetypal substratum to human consciousness, proposed that Spiritual or subconscious energy takes form in the mind as an archetype. In *Memories, Dreams, and Reflections,* Jung speaks of the human desire for Spirituality, our need for experiencing the eternal. "Meaning makes a great many things endurable—perhaps everything. No science will ever replace myth, and myth cannot be made out of any science for it is not that 'God' is a myth, but that myth is the revelation of a divine life in man."

According to Jung, archetypes found in our myths refer to inherited unconscious ideas, patterns of thought and images all people collectively hold to; they are universally present in our individual psyches. Caroline Myss, author of five *New York Times best sellers*, further develops this concept in her books: *Anatomy of the Spirit* (1996), *Why People Don't Heal and How They Can* (1998), *Sacred Contracts* (2002), *Invisible Acts of Power* (2004), *Entering the Castle* (2007), *Defy Gravity* (2009), and *Archetypes: Who Are You?* (2013).

Myss's book *Archetypes: Who Are You?* explores the intriguing subject of universal patterns of consciousness. Perceiving life as an archetypal theater, she echoes Shakespeare's poem "All the World's a Stage," in which everything we create in life as individuals, groups, and nations is associated with our cosmic patterns of consciousness, our archetypes.

Archetypes aren't all Greek mythological characters. They are original patterns or models, creational blueprints that trigger our behavior. They are our inner mysteries. Some therapeutic modalities refer to these as "surplus reality." They activate in certain situations through time and generations. They can make a real mess with our cells, shortening our lives and causing all kinds of havoc right outside our awareness in that part of our brain on autopilot. They live as characters in our minds, like our deceased relatives and people we haven't seen in years or never. We use them in metaphors and stories. They are our teachers when we act in relationship to them. Who knows, we may have even programmed them before we were born to arrive at a specific time in our lives. They urge us into a deeper life and inspire us through our waking and sleeping dreams—forms of our internal dialogue.

Our archetypal symbols are images and words—words that influence our internal makeup—words such as *beauty*, *love*, and *forgiveness*. They are words that represent a complete story or process, a code language of sorts. Our lives become the words and stories we repeat to ourselves. Words have the power to limit us or set us free. The childhood adage "Sticks and stones can break my bones but words will never hurt me" simply isn't true. Words can create fear, pain, depression, or courage and action. The choice is up to you. Yes, each of us assigns meaning to words based on our experience. Words make up our thoughts that manifest as our lives.

Words create certain images in our minds. (Even a black void or a cloudy space is an image.) Words are symbols of things, not the actual things. The word *tree*, for example, calls up a particular image in all of us. This image is probably out of awareness; nevertheless, it is an image. What image do you create when you think, *Tree*? Is it an image of a maple in the fall, a Christmas tree, a fruit tree, or maybe an oak? To understand this word, you made an image of several trees. We usually don't take time to think about what *kind* of tree. This is simply in the background to whatever else we are thinking. Some people conceive and express life in very concrete and specific terms, while others use abstract and general language. These two groups have difficulty communicating with each other; one is mired in the earth, and the other is lost in the heavens.

Our internal images communicate with each other, creating an inner structure similar to virtual reality. This structure becomes our inner world, our mental self, and it is the template for most of our perception of the physical world and our understanding of the Spiritual world. Our internal conflicts represent an opening for an archetype to move into our awareness and seek integration into our personality. The talents they open in our personalities manifest in the world, creating profound shifts in our unconscious and maturing us in our awareness of who we are. Our internal conflicts come from trying to repress this process.

We have a choice to remain in conflict, unaware of the archetypal forces pressing on us, or we can bring them into our consciousness and recognize their effects. When we do the latter, we move into a time of enormously exciting growth, which facilitates the release of newly found creative energy (yes, creative energy). Every mother and father integrates an aspect of their archetypal parent when they create a child—a completed gestalt, process that makes the sum of their parts, greater than their individual selves do.

There are many archetypal figures available for integration. However, regardless of our religious orientation, or lack of it, we who have grown up in America have inherited numerous archetypes of Judeo-Christianity as part of our mental substratum, and they eventually press to come into consciousness. In many cases, we have introjected them— swallowed the whole without chewing, contemplating, or analyzing. We accept them without question or reject them out of defiance rather than out of an informed choice.

All the mentioning of God, Jesus, Christ, Satan, Soul, and so forth, which occurs in the everyday language of Americans, annoyed my foreign friend while he visited the United States for six weeks. He described his annoyance as being similar to the annoyance many visiting Americans feel when noting his country's acceptance of in-your-face pornography. He reported that as a whole those in his country were atheists in practice. However, when approaching death, some embrace Catholicism, the state religion, to have a proper and dignified funeral.

After his visit, I too began to notice just how ubiquitous the language of Christianity is in our everyday comings and goings—in our profanity, our jokes, our doubts and wishes. Our inherited Judeo-Christian history became our cultural concepts. They live in the background of our existence, because they are part of our culture as Americans. I'm sure you've heard some of the following: "Well, for Christ's sake, stop doing that," "In the name of God, I beg you," "Oh, the devil made me do it," or "This godforsaken place." These familiar expressions create mental images in the minds of everyone growing up in America, regardless of his or her religious beliefs. Whether a Christian, an atheist, or agnostic, we all have "In God We Trust" on our American dollar, even if we refuse to say, "One nation under God."

Images created by words and carried in the background of our abstract thinking limit or enhance how we achieve or fail at life's tasks. Often we agree or disagree on a word's meaning. Each word's conceptual image contributes to the significance of our lives. Improper use of words can cause low self-esteem and failed relationships. Personal growth into our full selves comes through knowing what is going on in our silent thinking. Our task is to claim our own personal myths and surplus realities, and to manifest them physically in our everyday lives through awareness and choice.

Try drawing a picture that depicts each one of the following words, and you will discover that it takes many images to communicate it in a way someone can understand: *father, mother, heaven, hell, Satan, God, Book of Life, Soul, Christ, Savior, Spirit,* and *love.* If you live in America, you've heard all these words multiple times, regardless of any religious experiences or beliefs (or the lack of them). They are part of our cultural archetypes. Until we're able to control and manage the images these words produce—such as *God, Christ, Divine Child, Satan, hell, angels,* and others—we live in a junk heap of our minds, struggling to embrace or ignore them as we pray, protest, or deny.

Exercise 3: Some Judeo-Christian Cultural Archetypes

For later reference, take time to draw or make a note of what each of these images represents to you. Note any pictures, feelings, stories, or beliefs. Do you prefer one over the other?

God

Soul

Love

Satan

Jesus

Book of Life

What life experience helps you choose? Add any other words you would like to explore, such as the difference between *man, dad, daddy, girl, husband, wife, partner, mama,* and *mother.*

A preteen female, munching on cookies while on a road trip with her mother, commented, "Wow, these are really good cookies! What is in them?"

Her mother replied, "A lot of sin for sure."

The young passenger began reading the ingredient list, then responded, "No, Mom, there's no sin in these at all." She had no concept of the meaning of the word *sin*.

I tell this story frequently. Some reply, "How sweet that she doesn't know the meaning of *sin*." Others comment on how awful it is that her mother hasn't taught her about sin.

"She really needs to know what a sin is to keep her out of trouble."

We deal with all our mental images in a way that is sometimes detrimental and at other times beneficial. Without awareness, our response is the luck of the draw. We may have the illusion that we can hold these images outside ourselves and either treat them as locked-away objects and separate them from the working part of who we are or deify them as objects of our worship. Either way they become a problem until we integrate them into our whole selves.

A story my parents told to me as a child, as they recalled years of Sunday teachings from many versions of the Bible book of Revelations 12:9–12, uses cultural archetypal characters. My remembered version goes something like this:

> Once upon a time in a place called heaven, there was a magnificent cherub with a band of angel admirers. God had given him free will to choose his path with all the consequences that went along with each. This was the order of the

universe—the law of cause and effect. This cherub would answer when other angels called him "Star of the Morning, Son of the Dawn."

Fame, praise, recognition, and applause increased Star of the Morning, Son of the Dawn's sense of importance. He decided to take over the throne of heaven by overthrowing God. When the all-knowing God got wind of this, consequences followed; the illustrious cherub came to trial, which resulted in his demise. He was thrown out of heaven along with all his friends. The earth and its atmosphere became their primary abode of operations (Isa. 14:12–14). Since that day, Star of the Morning, Son of the Dawn and his followers are known as "Satan and his demons."

After this Satan, the master of disguise, master deceiver and tempter, prince of demons, and even master inventor of false knowledge, enhanced his disposition with hostility to all goodness, becoming the chief opponent to God, then to man. He didn't give up trying to conquer or persuade humankind to turn from goodness and join him (Luke 22:3). His aim is to undo the work of God (Mark 14:29), try to get man to denounce God, and bring about bereavement, sickness, and material loss (Acts 5:3). How was humankind to deal with such as this?

Listening with a child's ears, I heard the answer as, "God and the good angels love us. They can tell that we need some help to escape from the bad guys." The story continued.

God decided to send someone with opposite characteristics from those of Satan: a protector who would unconditionally love even the bad people. He would be peaceful, forgiving, nonjudgmental, accepting, validating, intuitive, creative, and purposeful. God couldn't just send a Spirit or an angel to help because recognition would be difficult for all those concrete thinkers. God decided to send his Son in the form of a man named Jesus. Because he was to live as a man, he would be able to stay only as long as his human body lived. God expanded his plan to protect humankind after Jesus' death by introducing the concept of Spirit.

God told Jesus he could leave his Spirit in the heart of humankind to help them discern the ways of Satan and resist being in despair. This was the Christ Spirit or the Holy Spirit, because he was from God. This plan helped some people who used their free will to choose the Christ way. However, others who failed to do anything came under Satan's power. Now, darkness overcomes all those who turn from the light.

This story planted archetypal images in my mind, later to be reconciled as I climbed Maslow's ladder. When was the first time you heard stories like this using any of these words? How does the use of the words *God, Satan, Jesus,* and *Christ* in this story compare to your images recorded in the previous exercise? If you think you've never heard them, how did the words have meaning for you? Could it be that your understanding results from your exposure to the archetypal words of Christianity and that you live in a society that uses them to communicate ideas beyond the boundaries of a religion or Spirituality?

The book titled *The Course of Miracles* chooses to use only two archetypes—fear and love or dark and light—and explains that dark is only the absence of light. Everyone deals with these symbols in some way. Of course, you may think you've simply dismissed them. Are you sure? Go ahead and try *not* to think of a pink elephant; you cannot. Your mind first creates a pink elephant and then erases it. Your mind may deal with the images from Christianity the same way.

The model A Sacred Trust: The Inner Child described in this book allows the creation of a new life and eventually the resolution of inner conflicts, leading you to embrace compassion and open you to your Spiritual possibilities. It is neither a religious model nor a nonreligious one. It provides a way of managing these archetypes rather than letting them manage you. This model works beautifully for my life and that of my clients. It brings the biblically described Spiritual structure of the universe into the mental structure and, in turn, the physical levels of living: heaven above manifesting below through the bridge of the mind. It views our Divine Child as sacred and entrusted to our developed, mature Nurturer's care and presence. Our Spirits heal through the faithful interaction between these two archetypal images. Spirit, mind, and body become one with the simple mental and physical enhancement of our own inner resources.

We do this by creating an internal significance through our voice and body for four of our culturally acquired Christian archetypes—Satan, Jesus, Divine Child, and Book of Life. We take these Christian images and give them their archetypal meaning and significance in our thinking and language. Then we physically manifest them as an expression in the world.

Rooms for Our Four Archetypes

Imagine that you can divide your thinking into four categories—four rooms of the mind representing four individual archetypes, if you will—and that every thought you have can be placed in one of these rooms. Wouldn't this step make managing your thinking a lot simpler?

In addition, by creating an expressive alliance through our bodies and voices for each of the four internalized archetype's, we build a pathway through our hearts of unconditional love for ourselves. This pathway of self-love loosens the boundary of our Souls, making visible our Spiritual presence in the world.

Exercise 4: Compartmentalizing Your Mind

Step 1: Take an eight-by-ten sheet of paper and let it represent your whole mind. Fill the complete page, letting the amount of your internal dialogue determine the relative size of four shapes: a rectangle, a square, a heart, and a star. Each shape or room will vary in size according to what you hear in your mind most of the time. (Some people have a huge room for one category, and the others are all very tiny. Other individuals have a difficult time filling the page.) Label each shape as follows:

1. A rectangle for your factual information and beliefs
2. A square box for your critical thoughts
3. A cloud or heart for your kind statements

4. A circle or star for your innermost feelings, referred to as your Wounded Child and later your Divine Child.

Step 2: Now, in each shape write the names of family members who characterized that shape. All the voices you recall fall in one shape/category or another. Take your time and listen. Some voices can speak to you from all categories. However, they all have their favorite. If you cannot decide which category they prefer, then place them in no more than two places. Uncle Harry might have taught you things and spoken to you kindly as well. He would go in your informational rectangle and your heart shape. Make each shape as full of as many names as possible. These are the people you hear inside you when you're alone or sitting, walking, driving, or trying to fall asleep.

Step 3: Notice which shape is the largest and how many names are in each shape. If you grew up in a very structured family with lots of rules, your critical shape will probably be the largest. (Initially, no one's Nurturer is ever the largest. If yours is, then rethink it.)

When we are too responsible as a child, our child section may be very tiny or have several other people's names in it other than our own. We were probably responsible for those other people in some way. If so, who was the child? How would you like all this to change? Do you want the informational container bigger or the one with kind voices to be fuller or both? (Clue: think about how you as a child would have liked your family to be different.)

How are you keeping yourself uninformed and depriving yourself of internal nurturing? You can restructure your inner system to allow the activation and nurturing of your whole self. First, you must choose to stop and really listen to your internal dialogue. When you do, you may notice that you're listening to recordings of voices that sometimes play constantly, while at other times the recordings will be of newly created voices. You may recognize your own voice as you silently speak, or the voice you hear in your mind may be someone else's voice, which you recorded long ago.

The voices may be soft, fast, or slow, loving or critical, intense or soothing. We splice these internal messages to create new conversations, or we record over them to create new dialogue and new ways of thinking. We also become misdirected, confusing the replay of someone else's speech for our own.

We also create pictures or movies to accompany these mental dialogues. Most of the time, these sounds and pictures play outside our conscious awareness, far in the background of our minds. Nevertheless, they play a significant part in how we choose to live out our lives. According to psychologist Carl Jung, all unconscious images—inherited unconscious ideas, patterns of thought, images, and so forth—are universally present in all our individual psyches.

Through careful listening, we begin to discover our own personal process of self-talk, the first step in creating a life of peace, joy, and satisfaction. In other words, this book is an instruction manual for upgrading an internal, antique, hand-cranked phonograph to a state-of-the-art device.

In the following metaphoric figure of a house, each shape represents a different room of the mind. Our free will determines the content of each room, as well as where and how each will influence our lives. We use our free will to choose which room of our mental house we will live in from moment to moment.

When we apply the function of each shape (room) in our metaphoric house to the following four basic culturally acquired Christian archetypal images, our mental chatter and confusion can cease to overwhelm us. (An explanation for each room is forthcoming in the following sections.)

1. Rectangle: Mentor (the Book of Life on earth)
2. Square: Critic (Satan, darkness; an obstacle to completing the process)
3. Heart or cloud: Nurturer or Divine Nurturer (Jesus, the man; Christ, the Spirit)
4. Circle or star: Divine Child (Soul fragment and blocked by your wounded inner Child)

Does giving labels to the previously drawn shapes change their size in your mind? As you learn to manage each mental division, you will begin to see how each affects your capacity to be true to yourself, the "you" you really are.

Humans have free will, so we can choose what we think and do in life. Most people fall into inertia, do nothing, believe their thoughts are out of their control, and allow their minds to lead them all over the place until they are totally lost. We give up our power of free will, our right and power to choose, when we (1) believe we cannot control our own thinking, (2) come under the influence of drugs or alcohol, or (3) decide to give our power over to someone else (including significant archetypes). Your mind creates the world as you perceive it.

Our sense of separation and power to choose came first through our understanding of language and the sense of the meaning of the word *me*. We increased our distance from others when we understood our *you* and finally our *I*. We must return to our young self (around age two) to the identity called *me* to reach the ultimate *I* and our own great *I am* our Soul. In exercise five, take your time and really notice your body's sensations for each pronoun. Each response will be different. Make a note of your answers for future references.

Exercise 5: From *You* to *I* to *Me*

- Where in your body are you when you're *you*?
- What age are you when you're *you*?
- Where in your body is your *I*?
- How old is your *I*?
- Where in your body is your *me*?
- How old is your *me*?

Once you stop splitting into *you* and *yourself*, there is no self. All is *you* in love. You're whole, an *I* of the *I Am*. "God said to Moses, 'I AM that I AM': and he said, 'Thus you shall say to the children of Israel, I AM has sent me unto you'" (Ex. 3:14).

An inscription on the Jefferson Memorial in Washington, DC, states, "Almighty God hath created the mind free. I have sworn upon the altar of God eternal, hostility against every form of tyranny over the mind of man" (Thomas Jefferson to Dr. Benjamin Rush, Monticello, September 23, 1800).

An anonymous tourist's responds, "God's grief must come by watching humankind sacrifice so much in the pursuit of personal freedom while expending so little in the pursuit of internal freedom; we have yet to escape the tyranny of our own minds" (2003).

Figure 8: Model for an Organized Mind

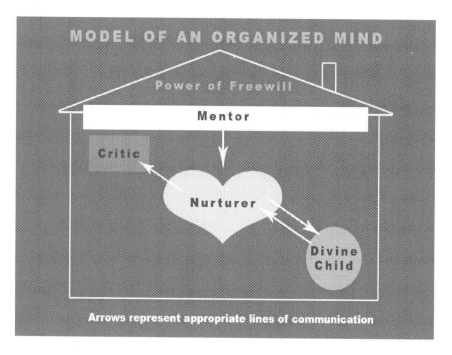

STEP 2

MENTOR

My Book of Life

...and another book was opened, which is the book of life: and the dead were judged out of those things what were written in the books, according to their works.

—Revelations 20:12

For as he thinketh in his heart, so is he...   —Proverbs 23:7

Table 1: The Mentor

Archetypal Representation
• The Book of Life, universal wisdom • Manages equal distribution of information.
Mental Construct
• Personal history, cognitive self, moral code
Physical Manifestation
• Neutral in relationship to people and events • Robotic vocal intonation patterns • Calm, relaxed body

THE MENTOR'S CHARACTERISTICS

- Stores factual constructive sequential data
- Accumulates beliefs and values (even when contradictory)
- Knows the positive intent of other dialoguing parts
- Speaks in an unemotional, robotic voice

ROOM 1

THE MENTOR

The Mentor, modeled after the archetypal Book of Life, holds all our values and beliefs, in addition to all the information we've acquired through living. This part is our conscious mind. The Mentor is self-reflective and with it, we can observe our own behaviors. It observes all our programmed behaviors when we engage in them. The conscious mind's capacity to override the subconscious mind's programmed behaviors is the foundation of free will (Lipton). In using our upcoming Mentor room of our minds, we heighten our awareness and exercise more choices through our free will.

Now, imagine that every bit of information about you in the world is in a sequential timeline in front of you, beginning on your left, when you were born, and ending on your right at your death. It is never erased or written over; it only makes additions.

Exercise 6: Timeline of Beliefs and Values

1. On a large sheet of paper, draw at the top a long horizontal line to represent your lifeline.
2. Place the date of your birth at one end and the age you expect to be when you die at the other.

3. Place a vertical line one-third of the space from the beginning and another line one-third of space from the end.

4. The first third of the line represents your life until age thirty, the second represents your life from thirty to seventy, and the last third represents the remaining years of your life.

5. In a column under each age category, beginning with the middle one (thirty to seventy years), list your values (example: honesty) and beliefs (example: dishonest shows a lack of integrity).

6. Divide the first section into three parts—ages two to six, ages seven to seventeen, and ages eighteen to thirty. List your values and beliefs under each age division. Add a note to indicate what occurred to give you that belief. Notice how your beliefs have changed.

7. In the final years of your timeline, list how beliefs may change or have changed again.

8. Notice how the changes occurred. Did you shift your perception about something?

The Mentor serves as that power from which we seek guidance. It is an ally of our higher selves. It supports the basic life purpose of our individuality without judgments or emotions. This positive part of ourselves makes unemotional, factual observations. It doesn't receive or generate the emotional sting that taints critical statements. The Mentor recognizes dysfunction or poor form without having a reaction to what it recognizes.

From the Mentor state of mind, you see and have a choice to update an action rather than to have an automatic, knee-jerk response from the position of judging. This creates a clear space for a loving presence. The Mentor is that part of you concerned with creating a more efficient, conscientious, and satisfying life. The Mentor archetype has the vision to manage the fair distribution of power in whatever form it takes.

It wakes you up without an alarm clock; it tells you when you've passed the exit on the freeway while daydreaming. Our Mentor contains all our values and beliefs, including those that are contradictory or filed "forgotten." It is the keeper of all our learned factual, unemotional data. It is the part of you that is reading this page as well as taking in and storing this information.

Our Mentor has recorded every conscious or unconscious experience we've ever had. Our mental strategy for remembering determines the perspective for most of our recordings. For example, recall the first thing you saw this morning when you opened your eyes. Most likely, you can remember this experience as though you were right there in your body, looking out through your eyes. Stop reading and try this experiment now.

What was the moment recorded *before* you opened your eyes? Is that moment stored through one of your other senses— sound, taste, smell?

Our childhood attitudes, beliefs, and memories often come into conflict with information gathered from our experiences as adults. For example, most of us believed Santa Claus was a real person living in our time until we started school and older kids told us otherwise.

If we were able to access only the first few years of recordings in our Mentor, we would still believe Santa lived at the north pole. As we mature, we shift to a more abstract perception that allows some of us to become Santa. We take on Santa's persona in the Spirit of Christmas. We successfully resolve our inner conflict between our childhood belief and our adult knowledge through a shift in perspective, a change in perception. We do this when we want to add new information or delete old, to learn new material, to resolve childhood pain or life traumas, and to improve our relating to other people.

Useful life information without an emotion is stored in the Mentor, such as how to discern. Discernment is required in trusting. Trusting is required in intimacy. Intimacy needs vulnerability. Vulnerability needs love.

There is no such thing as total across-the-board, wide-open trust. The Mentor in us needs to see the evidence that allows us to think, *I can depend on this person; I can trust this person.*

- When?
- Where—in what situations?
- How—predictable behavior?
- What—outcome?

Your response may be, "She always reads my mail when I leave it on the table. She borrows my clothes and returns them in worse shape. Therefore, I can trust her to violate my physical boundaries." Or: "She rescues me when others make negative remarks about what I am doing. I can trust her to protect me emotionally." Or: "He frequently has an unemotional opinion about my behavior when I drink too much, and he accurately discerns other people's behavior as well. Therefore, I can trust him to have an honest opinion, even if I don't like his opinion."

Our Mentor also helps us build good relationships. When we seek to build a new relationship, we need to be sure our Mentor is compatible with that of the other person's Mentor. Stored common life experiences and beliefs in the Mentor add to the compatibility and harmony of a relationship. Without this compatibility between the two Mentors, it's like trying to merge Apple with Microsoft. Among other things, there needs to be more information in each person's intellectual system for an enjoyable exchange to take place.

One of the theoretical concepts actors learn is the James-Lang theory. This concept places the body in a particular position or shape. Then the actor moves with these characteristics. Finally, the actor adds the voice that goes with the particular form and movement. This addition causes the natural feeling of the character to develop. All of us have done this at one time or another when we mimic someone.

Congruency of voice and feeling creates a believable character. By reading and participating in the following exercises, you will be able to experience the James-Lang theory for yourself as you create mind-body congruency. (This acting technique will be used later to help identify your different mental parts.)

This will bring the archetypal/Spiritual concept of the Book of Life into your mental awareness as the Mentor (left brain) and into a physical form through your body and voice (right brain). The Spirit manifests in the mind; the mind displays itself through the body; the body then walks in the Spirit, and so the circle goes.

Fritz Pearls, the father of Gestalt therapy, is reported to have said, "Get out of your head and into your body" when he thought people were over intellectualizing the moment. So, let us move from our thinking and begin to experience the physical sensations of the Mentor body. This physical manifestation of our Mentor is useful when we want to be emotionally detached from a situation. We can avoid fear at a job interview or an interrogation by whomever. In this mind-set, our emotional life is private. We appear poised, confident, and in control. Your skill in using your Mentor mind and body is essential before moving on to the next mind-set.

Exercise 7: Mood Control or Warm-Up

Practice this acting technique several times. This skill is used later to construct the other rooms of the mind.

Step 1: Place your body in the position of being happy, erect, healthy, alive, and energetic. Sit or stand straight and put a smile on your face, even if you don't feel like it. Look up while keeping your head level and focus your eyes slightly to the right as you make a mental picture of an enjoyable event anticipated in the future. Stop reading and do this now.

Step 2: Once you complete Step 1, keep the same posture and pleasant thought. Begin to move as a happy, joyful person moves; and as you do, add a sound by using words, a song, a poem, or anything a happy person would say. Once again, stop reading; experience this.

Step 3: Do you feel happier, more joyful, or excited when you do this than when you started? If you aren't sure, exaggerate the posture and movement even more. Dance around the room, swinging your arms while singing louder. Continue until the initial resistance or foolish feeling is past and you can genuinely feel happy. Remember to keep your eyes focused upward, while you reach up and out with your hands.

Exercise 8: Out of Your Mind, into Your Body: Your Mentor's Physical Form

Step 1: Begin by standing or sitting tall. Let go of any facial expressions. Using a normal tone of voice, repeat your name, address, and phone number three times aloud.

Step 2: Repeat this again in front of a mirror until you can do this successfully without any facial expression. You should feel neutral as if bored, and you should be speaking from rote memory. Notice this physical sensation in your body. Pay close attention to this sensation. This is the sensation of your newly created mental boundary or compartment called the Mentor, and this is your body and voice that go with it.

Over the next several days, notice when you're in your Mentor mind and body. You will have that neutral overall sense of control; be absent of any opinions, emotions, or judgments. The Mentor is your personal container for all information you observed and recorded over your life's span, only the facts. This is your omnipotent observer, your objective listener, as you move along to the most familiar and currently largest room of the mind, the Critic.

Be assured and confident that your Mentor will (1) keep you on the right path while remaining calm and unafraid, (2) collect and store the information you need for a better life, and (3) sort all your internal dialoguing into the right four categories.

Over the next week, make what you're doing in your mind more interesting to you than what is happening to you. Become the court reporter of your mind, your thoughts, your reactions to your thoughts, and your emotions. Stay in the present moment, not the past or the future. Don't judge or praise, be simply the recorder of your life's events and, in so doing, feel the power of detachment.

STEP 3

CRITIC

The Devil Made Me Do It

Beloved, believe not every Spirit, but test the spirits whether they are of God because many false prophets are gone out into the world.
—1 John 4:1

A wholesome tongue is a tree of life: but perverseness therein is a breach in the Spirit. —Proverbs 15:4

Table 2: The Critic

Archetypal/Spiritual Correlation
• Judge (shadow), Satan, evil, darkness, separateness
Mental Construct • Disguised as people we know and love • Destructive self-criticism, male or female voice • *Should/ought* language, accusing, blaming, judging; lacks empathy • Abusive to other mental parts • Active when we are silent, asleep or thinking
Physical Manifestation • Tension: restriction in energy flow • Personal suffering, destruction, disease, depression • Pseudopower

The Critic's Characteristics

- Is incapable of love and guiltless
- Can appear unexpectedly
- Attempts to gain recognition, to remain important
- Eavesdrops on and interrupts other mental processes
- Creates personal suffering, destruction
- Holds the illusion of separateness and despair

ROOM 2

THE CRITIC

Although neutral in essence, archetypes may manifest as having both light and dark characteristics. The dark characteristics of the archetypal judge belong to our Critic. For most of us, our Critic is our largest, most vocal compartment. Soon after our birth with the loss of innocence, we find ourselves thrown out of the archetypal garden of Eden to live in an imperfect world. A child struggling to survive embraces the law of the land, the law of cause and effect; the child creates a Critic, an active part that ensures survival. Developing a Critic is a natural process as we grow into a human adult. However, the mechanism that keeps us safe as a child becomes a destructive process as the adult. The bigger our Critic grows, the more our spontaneity and excitement to create diminish. Our wonderment and excitement of childhood seem lost.

Suppressed creativity creates imbalance and conflict in our adult lives. The Critic grows from our original pain and confusion from childhood and continues to grow due to our lack of effort as adults to employ our free will to restrain it. As adults, how we manage our Critic determines the outcome of our lives and the kind of world in which we live.

We are now in the time of choice, the time for activating our free will to choose between love and fear, light and dark. On which team are we going to play? Not deciding leaves us on the bench, and being left on the bench automatically places us on the dark team, because we gave up our free will of choice. This unchecked internal voice of the Critic is a demon of destruction for us spiritually, mentally, emotionally, and physically. The Critic keeps all our emotions, desires, thoughts, and sensations that come from within isolated, hidden, or suppressed.

Our Critic functions similarly to a big rubber stopper plugging up an opening, keeping the creative waves of our life expression locked inside. When we push the Critic aside, we're free to create our new reality and change our existence. Our perceptions of our past change; we remember it differently. Our illusions of fear, grandeur, or defeat disappear, and the Critic loses its illusion of power.

Like the genie in Aladdin's lamp, the voices from the room labeled "Critic" can appear like magic, taking form out of nothing and floating on the abyss of our minds like smoke. These voices can be active when we are silent, when we are talking, and even when we are asleep. They impersonate any face and voice to which we are vulnerable, as in the movie *The Exorcist*, when the satanic use of the voice of the priest's mother pulls him away from the light. The Critic is a master of self-deception—one moment being illustriously beautiful while the next being pitifully mangled and dejected. It is a cheat and a liar, a wolf in sheep's clothing. It can, in the name of God, portray the best of religion or philosophy while cheating life and denying God. Even though it may say it intends well, it is an unknowing ally of the dark side of life. Emotions of fear or dread and sometimes anger signal the presence of a disguised Critic.

As children, to ensure our survival, we learned our household rules (introjects) and how to conform. Rules like "Look both ways before crossing the street" were and still are beneficial. However, it is through this process that we created our Critic. The Critic uses words such as *should, must, have to, ought to, supposed to, needed to, stupid, dumb,* and many other negative statements and tones of voice. It usually uses the voice of a critical parent, a mate, a boss, or someone with authority who wants to be in control by demanding better. Keep in mind that this internal voice, even though it sounds familiar, is a product of our own making and not of society's. It is a product of our development, and each of us is responsible for its continued influence in our lives. It is in your mind. However, the internal words of *should* and so forth to which you respond is someone else's rule and belief. When we chew on them, they become part of us, and the rule becomes our values or our beliefs. It sounds like "I want to" or "I intend to."

Self-criticism is the primary tool used to dominate the other parts of our thinking. The older we get, the worse the condition becomes. Think of all the times your self-doubts or criticisms have kept you from experiencing your heart's desire. A tremendous amount of creative energy is lost through swallowed criticisms—introjects. This loss creates a sense of overall self-impoverishment and low self-esteem. Anxiety, guilt, doubt, shame, and depression are oppressive experiences generated by self-criticism, which restricts creative energy and play. The restricted creative flow leaves us lonely inside and isolated. A longing for a Nurturer, a Spiritual ally, emerges.

The Critic rejects, discounts, criticizes, judges, condemns, punishes, argues, and destroys. We mistakenly give it the position of power and authority within our minds, and it becomes a slave driver, inflicting internal psychological abuse—mental anguish.

The Critic uses harmful ideas or beliefs to control our behavior. Mental statements such as "Feelings aren't acceptable," "No one wants to hear bad news," "People can't handle me," "If I get close to someone, one of us will die," "People outside the family can't be trusted," and "Talking about sex is a no-no" are examples of critical introjects created from childhood beliefs that limit our adult expression.

The way our family interacted, nurtured, and disciplined is our internal model of operation. It is the template for how our mind continues to work. Mentally, we treat ourselves the same way we were treated while growing up. What was missing then is still missing now, unless we redraw our mental design into a form that produces a sense of completeness in ourselves.

Technically, the Critic is a projection of our disowned parts, assigned to an image of someone held in our minds and heard as another's voice. A projection is taking place anytime we put our own attitude onto another person and then say that this person *makes* me feel thus and so. When we experience conflict due to our internal dialoguing, then the conflict is between two parts of ourselves. We align with one part and alienate another simply by saying, "The Devil made me do it" or by blaming our mother, father, or the government. Try using "I statements" and see what happens—"I made me do it." Who is my *I* and who is my *me*? (Yes, you split yourself in half. Don't worry; we are in the process of getting you wholly together.)

When you imagine the future, what component of the present do you use to begin? An image of your house, car, a location, or a body sensation? Do you first think about how these things are now and then how you would like them to be in the future? Then do you take action steps to make them happen, or do you stop yourself with your fears?

Our hopes and wishes come from our Spirit seeking expansion. What do you usually do with your hopes, your wishes? What choice do you make with your free will? Does your fear keep your hopes and wishes locked safely in a box by aligning with your Critic and therefore creating what you're afraid of in an attempt to justify your past existence? We are unaware of our subconscious programs because our conscious mind is busy with hoping and wishing. We make statements such as, "See, I knew I wouldn't win" or "I was afraid that would happen." They give us clues about what is going on in our subconscious. What we fear we create to give ourselves the opportunity to develop the skills to overcome that fear. Your future depends on you, your thoughts, your dreams, and your actions. The following exercise will help you do something different; use your free will to align your dream with your creative actions to make them your reality.

Exercise 8: Creating Your Hopes and Wishes

Materials: Five sheets of paper, pencil, crayons, and a large paper clip or staples

Step 1: Assign a number to each sheet of paper (1, 2, 3, 4, 5) and then set them aside. Fill in the following labeled spaces with a word for each section and the fears that get in the way of your actions.

Hopes and Wishes   Actions Needed

1.

2.

Fears That Could Interfere with Actions

1.

2.

Step 2: Symbols

Read A–C aloud and record what you say. Then play them back, listen, and respond.

A. Now close your eyes and imagine a circle in the middle of your forehead. Color it purple.

B. Allow the circle to become larger and larger until you can float in the circle. Kick back and float in your hopes and wishes.

C. Allow a symbol to rise out of your purple circle that represents your number one hope or wish. Take your time. Enjoy ... and release (allow thirty seconds to pass). Now, open your eyes. Draw and color your circle on paper number one.

D. Quietly close your eyes and allow a second symbol to appear to represent your fear of achieving this hope and wish. Draw the symbol of your fear on paper number two.

E. Again, close your eyes and allow a third symbol to come that represents the actions needed to overcome your fear and manifest your number one hope and wish. Draw this symbol on paper number three.

Read F aloud and record it. Play it back, listen, and respond.

F. Close your eyes and imagine an image of a container, such as an empty bowl, a box, a trunk ... to appear that can hold the symbol of your fears, that can keep them contained so you can take the action needed to achieve your hopes and wishes ...
    Open your eyes.
G. Draw the container on paper number four.

Read H—I aloud and record your words. Play it back and listen and respond.

H. Take your time and imagine the purple circle from Step A. Allow it to show you a glimpse of your number one hope and wish successfully achieved in your future.
I. Leave your purple circle and return to present time as you notice the change in your physical sensation. Open your eyes. Draw your successful achievement on paper number five.
J. Write a description of your sensations.

Step 3: Place the container drawing (number four) over the fearful one (number two). Now, place the action drawing (number three) on top of the container drawing (number four).

Finally place the achievement drawing (number five) on top of the action drawing (number four over two, number three over four, and number five over three). Notice the difference between your symbols: one of a hope or wish (number one) and of successful achievement or manifestation (number five) of that hope or wish. Use drawing number five as your motivation to continue with actions. Now in present time, within thirty-six hours, take one initial action needed to begin the manifestation of your dream.

Posture of the Critic

The defensive posture of the Critic extends from our inner world to the outer world. The Critic manifests as fear, immobility, and indecisiveness. The Critic works to avoid pain and in doing so creates the paradox of constantly creating internal suffering in us through deception and repression or by splitting off parts of our mind and body. The Critic uses our internal suffering to manipulate others, to get its own way, to glorify itself, or to have a means of indulging in self-pity or guilt. (It makes our inner Child whine and beg.) It can see others as only a support or threat to its existence. This view, in turn, hinders real contact and denies meaningful relationships. This process also prevents integration of the personality and the moving into wholeness. We are isolated in our own darkness. Addiction is an example of the Critic in action, affecting the lives of others for generations.

Another way the Critic feeds suffering is by creating an individual who plays the martyr. When we allow the mental process of becoming a victim of our Critic, we project, and we envision others to be persecutors. In turn, the world accommodates this internal dynamic, and we encounter persecutors in our environment. We may even become paranoid and live in an illusion rather than in and from ourselves.

A successful client of mine was in fear of losing his license due to his excessive vodka drinking. While in school, he used alcohol to reduce his awareness of his need for rest and told himself it was a reward for long hours of work. (Who do you think was talking?) His Critic continued the pressure with, "You should be able to handle the demand" and "What's wrong with you, you wimp?"

After graduating, he and his professional wife continued to suppress their real needs with alcohol to reach their practice goals. When they began to feel successful in reaching their goals, they drank even more to celebrate. They called themselves "social drinkers." In reality, they drank to sedate the cry of the denied real self. Then an interesting thing began to happen, as it always does, when we are resistant to our own need to change. He intensified his projecting of his critical voices onto his wife. He heard negativity in any little thing she said and responded from his Critic. "You should be more appreciative of me. You're always demanding more of me. Give me a break."

She decided she wasn't going to live with someone who was so negative and discontented. After all, she was successful too and deserved more joy. She filed for divorce and moved on. He overdosed with drugs and alcohol, failed to go to work for three days, and ended up in the hospital with a diagnosis of depression. In an effort to keep his license, he then came to see me so he could say he was in treatment for depression rather than for an addiction.

When his work schedule changed or he felt mistreated in any way, he went home and drank himself into a stupor. His excuse was always, "I needed it to sleep, and I really like vodka. It's my only comfort. All the men in my family drank vodka when they came home from work. I don't drink and drive, and I don't drink when I'm on call. I am not an alcoholic." The only relationship he had internally was one with criticism.

He began to realize that the only relationship he had was with his bottle of vodka. He had little ability to nurture himself. At that point, he began to ask "Why?" After several weeks, he was able to own the fact that he needed vodka to quiet the critical voices in his mind. He didn't know anything else to do, and he was afraid of being caught with a high alcohol level at work.

We experience life as humans through our bodies—a rare gift. Our bodies carry the potential for self-knowledge, self-healing, love, and compassion. By reawakening our perceptive skills of feeling, sensing, and initiating, we allow the wisdom of the body to emerge, to guide and inform us. Opportunity for choice comes through awareness. Some Gestalt therapists claim that awareness is 95 percent of the cure.

Like the Mentor, the Critic takes physical form through our choice of words, tone of voice, and body movements. We become more aware of our Critic as we engage in the process of identifying its physical characteristics. The following exercise helps to locate your dis-ease in your body, which in turn gives you an opportunity to choose to change.

Exercise 9: Identifying Your Critic

Step 1; Take some time to make a list of critical or negative statements that easily come to mind, such as, "How could you do that?", "You stupid _____!", or "That's not right." Make your own personal critical list. Make the list as extensive and critical as your memory will allow.

Step 2: While listing your critical remarks, take time to repeat each phrase aloud. Note the gender, male or female, of each mental voice that expresses a particular phrase. For example, a male is more likely to say, "You bitch!" "You bastard!" may come from a female voice.

Step 3: Next, note the created emotion. Use only the four basic feelings—glad, sad, mad, and afraid—as descriptive emotional words.

Step 4: Note which part of your body holds the tension the critical remark creates. If you're still unsure, look in the mirror as you speak.

Janice McDermott, M.Ed., LCSW

Personal Critical Remarks

Even though we may contribute all these statements to someone else, we are the ones generating them in our minds in the moment. They are recordings that belong to our Critic. They are the messages we play again and again inside our heads, and the person listening to them is another part of us. The Critic is like an over exercised muscle; it was developed through excessive use. A part of yourself remains dominant from childhood because your parents' own Critics intimidated you. You hid some part of yourself from the world to guarantee your survival. This fact is true for all of us.

Now *we* replay these internal, negative messages and hide parts of ourselves from ourselves. Subsequently the world loses the gifts these parts intended to deliver. When the message begins to fade, we most likely substitute our own voice or the voice of a current acquaintance. As you go throughout your day, notice when you hear yourself have a critical thought; make a note of it and add it to your previous Personal Critical Remarks. List *all* critical possibilities—discover yourself. The most persistent force you will deal with is the Critic.

The previous-mentioned professional client discovered that he had long suppressed his heart's desire to be a swim coach. He wanted to give up his practice. "After all that time, money, and hard work to become a significant player in the health profession, how could you be so stupid?" remarked his Critic again and again, louder and louder, until quieting his mind became his main reason for drinking.

He worked with all these exercises until he was able to give himself his heart's desire. Now he uses his professional training to coach his own swim team. Currently addiction free, he enjoys a committed relationship and is happy in the way he spends his time. Can you imagine that? (The misdirected longing for truth found in the addict finds direction through A Sacred Trust: The Inner Child process. Wholeness becomes a choice rather than a goal.)

Exercise 10: Body and Voice

Note: With the body and voice performing as your Critic, another part of you may be listening and responding with fear. Just do an "aside" self-talk from your Mentor to your "afraid listener." Tell this listener that you're pretending to rehearse a play and not to listen.

Step 1: Now choose one of the remarks from your completed Personal Critical Remarks chart. Say it aloud while finding the appropriate voice and body posture that fits the tone of voice for this remark. Speak loudly, exaggerating your posture and facial expression. Become this character.

Step 2: As you hear yourself say these negative words, notice whether your body tenses—tightened jaw, stiffened shoulders, and/or hardened face. Intensify these body parts a little more as you turn up the volume of your Critic. (Please, don't think you can do this silently.) You may feel your energy begin to move you to point your finger in an accusing manner, to put your hands on your hips with determination, or to slam your hand down on a hard surface. As you take on a posture, increase the volume and speed of your speech. Exaggerate your movements. Go over your edge until your words and body become one. Use all your internal energy. Let go! Feel the release.

Step 3: Continue by saying aloud any of the statements from your Personal Critical Remarks chart you remember hearing other people say, such as, "Why don't you grow up?", "Hurry up!", "You should never have been born," or "How can you be so stupid?" Feel your energy and intensify it. (Don't look in the mirror this time. You'll scare yourself.)

Step 4: Make sure your body posture is overt enough that you can feel the change. Increase your volume, speed, and the intensity of your voice until there's congruency between your repeated remark, your body, and your voice. (Pretend you're an actor in a play. Stop reading and complete this step. Win that Academy Award!)

Step 5: Once you've achieved the above steps, quickly repeat another selected remark. Notice how you feel in your body and how you feel emotionally. Record these feelings in your Personal Critical Remarks list if you haven't done so already. It is imperative that you actually experience this process in your body rather than merely read about it. Practice this Critic until you're aware of the feeling in your body, even when not speaking your mental dialogue aloud.

Step 6: Reverse the process. Notice your body tension first (how you're feeling) and then match your tension to internal dialogue. Turn up the volume on your mental dialogue so you can hear what is said through your body, even when you aren't paying attention to your thoughts.

Step 7: Now, listen carefully and notice when the critical voice comes on in your mind and the accompanying overt body posture isn't visible. If you only go through the motion in your life without passion in the moment for what you're doing, you're guilty of being one of the "people of the lie" Scott Peck described in his book *People of the Lie.* Please stop and complete this exercise before you continue reading.

With increased listening awareness, you will be able to push the OFF button before your Critic can gain too much power or control over your body. You may also benefit by recording yourself as you repeat this exercise. Notice your tone of voice as you listen to it from your Mentor. Do you sound believable? (Be sure to remind other listening mental compartments that you aren't talking to them.)

When we explore criticisms in general, we can find that some are instructive, others are constructive, still others are destructive, and some are entirely beside the point. Only the Critic contains destructive criticism, expressed in numerous ways. Such messages are especially hurtful because they reinforce the bad feelings we may already have about ourselves. As a result, the oppressed Divine Child withdraws from a hurtful situation. It is through this kind of criticism that we interrupt our sense of play. When this happens, we lose our spontaneity, creativity, and self-esteem. Pain results.

Take the next week to listen to and identify those tones of voice in others that indicate the presence of a Critic. Listen at the supermarket, school, work; and with family and friends. You also may hear people passing out "warm prickles," those statements that hide negativity in warm words. For example,

"You have really nice legs; bet you wish you were taller." The "warm prickles" statement causes you to lower your internal defense and to feel nourished by the incoming compliment, only to be stabbed in the gut by the negative remark riding in on the tail of the good one.

On the other hand, you may hear a "cold fuzzy" instead. It sounds like this: "Oh! Darling, you're just one of those unlucky people born without a personality, but I love you anyway." In this situation, we keep our internal defenses up to protect ourselves from the critical comment of the cold fuzzy only to find ourselves closed off and unnourished by the positive remark at the end.

Both "warm prickles" and "cold fuzzies" are destructive to our self-esteem. Are you guilty of making any of these kinds of statements to yourself? This is also a technique of your Critic. By the end of the week, you'll have a heightened awareness and a greater ability to spot the lurking Critic. In the process, you'll be adding new information to your Mentor. So listen up!

Remembering someone's voice saying these critical remarks over and over is the same as if you were saying them to yourself. Mentally use your free will to make a choice and listen in your mind only to those things that help you feel peace and love. Kindly tell your Critic to stop talking to you.

Don't engage in an extensive dialogue with your Critic or kick it out. Angry, harsh words or malice toward your Critic just means you've split it in half. Now you have two Critics. This is what happens when you try to throw out your negative self or argue with it. When you think you're completely clean and perfect, your dark side emerges bigger than ever, as described in Matthew 12:43–44. "When the unclean Spirit is gone out of a man, he walketh through dry places, seeking rest, and findeth none. Then he saith, 'I will return to my house from which I came out; and when he is come, he finds it empty, swept, and garnished.' Then goes he, and taketh with himself, seven other spirits more wicked than himself, and they enter in and dwell there, and the last state of that man is worse than the first."

ANGER

Repressed anger is damaging because we project it onto others. Through the influence of our education system, our church, the media, and our family, we learn to project our anger by denying the experiences of our body, acts of aggression against ourselves. By disassociating from the rushes of our excitement we experience through our bodies, we create a struggle within us that tends to spill out into other areas of our lives. In this process, we are vulnerable to being only a short step away from acts of aggression toward the environment and others. No matter how sweet the tone of voice or how positive the intent, destructive criticism creates psychic pain. Unresolved psychic pain results in conflict in some way. When we project our internal conflict, our anger, into the world, it can collectively manifest as nuclear war, terrorism, crime, race, and religious strife or any other major issue. We may even participate in or support these activities rather than looking inward to ourselves for the eradication of the cause of our anger and violence.

Figure 9: Repressed Anger

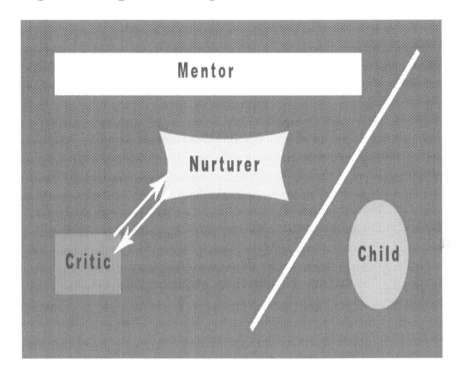

The Child needs a Nurturer to do the following:

1. Remove barriers between Nurturer and Child
2. Increase activity in Child (free Child)
3. Increase sensory awareness

There are three basic approaches to stopping violence. First, the world approach chooses to define the energy as nuclear war, terrorism, drugs, crime, race, and religious strife or any other major issue. Those who continue to place blame for war and violence on others and deny personal responsibility avoid their own anger, which is often a mask for their insecurity. Some of us try to manage our anger through the social approach by participating in or organizing social programs, such as job training and prison reform, to eradicate the supposed causes of violence. However, the root of our anger requires the third approach; we use the personal approach to work with our own aggression in our daily lives. When we deny or repress our own anger, we fail to take responsibility for what it produces in the world, and it will produce something externally. The task is to learn to live in peace with all parts of self—even the Critic. Then we will live in peace with others.

Once projected, our anger can take several forms. One is self-righteous judgment. We become self-righteous with the projection of what we judge to be bad about ourselves onto others. We are the judge in relationship to others. We judge with comments such as, "Who do they think they are?" When we hide our aggression behind self-righteousness, we metaphorically sit on the church's front pew and feel superior to others with our right and wrong judgment. In this state, the nurturing aspect of the self is bound in an energy knot. The Wounded Child is acting out. This is the composition of bullies. There is no love in this process. A phobia (projected fear of our emotional pain) is associated with aspects of ourselves we prefer to deny by projecting them onto others. Actually, we can even experience catastrophic fears of rejection when we see our feared parts in others. When we project ourselves onto others, we avoid responsibility for our own feelings and remain powerless to initiate change. We whine and complain, we become afraid of our own shadow, and when taken to an extreme, we may think that we're someone else and that others are going to persecute us (paranoid schizophrenia). On the other hand, we can become self-righteous, projecting what we think to be bad about ourselves onto others.

When we introject the archetypes of Christianity, becoming a slave to religion, we bind up our energy by following the rules without question. We react to God and others in a stereotypical and inauthentic way as we try to live up to our own, or other people's, fantasies of us. Our Divine Child gets lost in role-playing and games. We are only in a pretend form with no manifestation of our own Spirituality. We are phony. These introjects are found in the Critic or in the pretend facade of the Wounded Child. There is no equal exchange of Soulful energy. We die a slow Spiritual death. The Soul is lost in this impasse of self-righteous anger.

Figure 10: Self-Righteous Anger

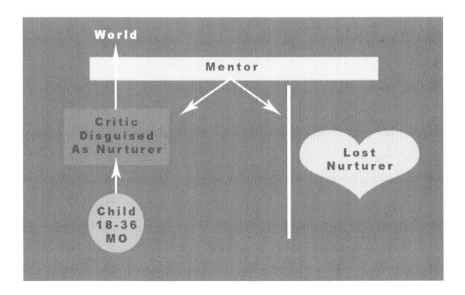

The Child needs a Nurturer to do the following:

1. Separate Child from Critic
2. Take power from Child by encouraging Child to surrender
3. Support Child in getting needs met
4. Encourage spontaneous giving and nurturing or loving

Life lived from the self-righteous Critic is negative, uncreative, and at times filled with critical rage. Self-righteous anger focuses on making other people wrong for their behaviors, feelings, or opinions. It blames or analyzes the other person ("You're too needy!" or "You're so depressed!") or assumes to know the motives of others ("You're just trying to get back at me!" or "You only care about yourself!"). These are intense, critical "you" statements. With intensity, self-righteousness becomes critical rage. (In the next room of the mind, we will develop a mature Nurturer, which gives us the support needed to go through this impasse and feel alive again.)

Repressed, nonintegrated anger moves from self-righteousness or paranoia to the physical expression of critical rage and uncontrolled anger. Critical rage continues to make other people wrong for their behaviors, feelings, or opinions. Critical rage is a high-energy physical response to a person or situation that threatens our Wounded Child, which in turn uses the Critic as a defense; it is a crack in our inner-anger container, a dam breach. A flood of uncensored words and actions, similar to the behavior of a two-year-old, rages forth.

Through choice of words, tone of voice, body movement, or expressions, we hear the unspoken message behind critical statements, such as "You're wrong. Don't you know anything?"

These kinds of messages say, in effect, "You aren't a worthwhile human being; you don't deserve love and respect." Tinged with personality attacks or judgmental inflections, they produce an explosion in the child part of our adult selves that is expressed through the Critic in a most destructive way. Critical rage creates fear and pain. Critical rage hurts. We choose to continue to use the rage of our angry Child as fuel to engage our Critic. Remember, we only have a choice when we consciously engage our free will otherwise; the dark team of the Critic uses us.

Figure 11: Critical Anger or Rage

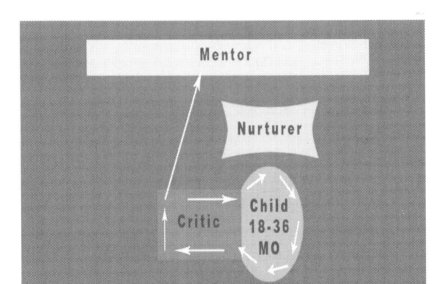

The Child needs the Nurturer to do the following:

1. Take control through compassion and authority
2. Create and control the boundaries between Critic and Child
3. Teach the Child self-containment

There is a huge difference between critical rage and constructive anger. Constructive anger is the kind Jesus expressed when dealing with the money-changers in the temple. Constructive anger reveals one's true feelings and unfulfilled needs uncontaminated by blame or guilt-producing statements. It is the caring expression of the adult Nurturer combined with the protective stance of the adult Mentor; both enable the godliness and sovereignty of the Divine Child to exist. Constructive anger moves us to act on our own behalf by either defending ourselves or removing ourselves from the situation.

Constructive anger is a healthy response to something unacceptable to the human Spirit. It defines our personal boundary. It helps us either to move toward the offender or to move away. It is an emotion and a behavior. For example, we can express constructive anger in the following manner: "I am infuriated with you for taking my _____. Return it now!" The emotional intensity in one's voice is the result of a passionate feeling expressed through the Nurturer and the Mentor rather than through the Critic. We need to make sure our words, tone of voice, and gestures aren't those of the Critic. And we need to be clear about which way we're moving—away from or toward—with the intent to remove something or someone from our sanctuary or ourselves from a situation. Keep in mind that your self is never an appropriate object for your own anger. When we are angry with ourselves, we're retroflecting and not completing the Gestalt process.

Figure 12: Constructive Anger

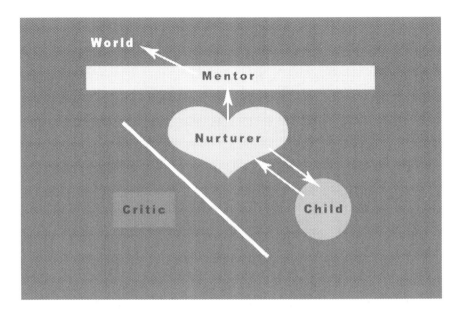

The Child needs the Nurturer to do the following:

1. Listen to the Child's discontent
2. Instruct the Child in appropriate ways of getting need met
3. Create with the Child an agreeable and appropriate action
4. Address the situation externally through the Mentor's voice and body toward an external person or situation

A genuine feeling of anger frequently begins with a feeling of having been hurt. When we're hurt, we feel sad, even though the sadness may not be in our awareness. Then we move from sadness into anger. When someone refuses to claim his or her feelings of hurt or sadness but can only display anger, then the use of anger is a defensive maneuver intended to reap revenge by frightening or hurting the other person rather than an expression of genuine emotion. We can never really know to what degree emotionally to trust ourselves with someone until we have seen that person's expressions of anger. Can he or she manage anger in an appropriate way? Is his or her anger a danger to others? Does he or she dump and attack or state his or her position with intense passion? Is he or she willing to change the way he or she expresses anger so as not to incite others' fears?

The Mentor's voice and body best express true anger in the present moment and situation. It is an impulse to push away the other person or ourselves and an expression of the mentor, Nurturer, and Divine Child working together, supporting each other. This kind of anger is never manipulative. If a stranger at the mall harmed a child in your care, you would automatically move to protect the child and then act to deter the offender. This is the same process to use with an internal offender of your inner Child.

Instead of making someone else wrong or fortifying a position that makes us right, we can work with what is most common and closest to all of us: our bodies, thoughts, emotions, feelings, and actions. We can personally work with our anger and aggression in our own lives. "Let there be peace on earth and let it begin with me" (song by Jill Jackson Miller and Sy Miller, 1995). Peace begins within our minds and bodies. By working sincerely and directly within our present bodily felt condition, we can affect our lives and the lives of others. When we heal ourselves, we heal others; we heal the world.

Assuming you have sufficiently explored your Critic and can identify its presence, you can now set it aside (not throw it out) and begin to discover your Nurturer, your loving self.

STEP 4

NURTURER

Getting the Love You Deserve

But Jesus called them unto him, and said, Suffer little children to come unto me and forbid them not: for such is the kingdom of God.

—Luke 18:16

Whosoever shall receive one of such children in my name, receives me: and whosoever shall receive me, receives not me, but him that sent me.   —Mark 9:37

Table 3: The Divine Nurturer

Spiritual Correlation • Love, life, Christ, God
Mental Construct • Unconditionally loving, supportive thoughts • Most powerful (when allowed to be present)
Physical Manifestation • Loving voice, kind words • Bodily ease, soft eyes • Sense of expansion and warmth • Peace, trust, positive actions

The Nurturer's Characteristics

- Buffers the effects of the Critic
- Is nonjudgmental, accepting, and validating
- Is unconditionally loving, even to the Critic
- Is peaceful, forgiving, protective, and instructive
- Is purposeful, intuitive, and creative

ROOM 3

DIVINE NURTURER

L ove moves us in one direction. Fear and anger move us in the opposite direction. Which way do you want to go? Where is your loving self? We like to think of ourselves as being nurturing, and often we are. However, acting in a nurturing manner to others and being nurturing to ourselves isn't the same thing. The emptiness or loneliness many adults experience is due to the absence of their Nurturer, the counterpart to the Critic. Low self-esteem, procrastination, and lack of productivity are further evidence of an underdeveloped Nurturer. Similar to an over exercised muscle, our Critic gets bigger and bigger, because we exercise it, while the Nurturer remains dormant from lack of development. Internally, we are out of balance.

You may have had parents who said all the right "I love you" words, but because they said them from the unemotional Mentor, you never felt the love. Their love lived in another room, too afraid to come out or too little to show up. In repeating their process, you continue to withhold love from yourself. However, you can change.

Growing an internal Nurturer is a new process for most people and requires paying significantly more attention to one's self as well as practice. Practice before you go to sleep, before you open your eyes upon awakening, and while walking and listening—most of all when listening to yourself. It takes nine months to grow a baby, so expect a similar length of time before birthing an automatically functioning internal Nurturer.

We all need more than we have received. As children, we have limited awareness of our psychological needs and limited means for expressing them. Adults in charge of our care guessed at what our needs were. They didn't always guess right. Consequently, as previously described, we created our internal Critic to keep our behavior in line—to survive physically. Our mothers embrace the duties of our initial nurturing even before we are born. As we mature into adulthood, we continue to perceive the Nurturer as located outside of us in someone else, first the mother or another caregiver and eventually a spouse or a significant other. The Nurturer located outside the self delays the development and expression of our talents and gifts—our unique expression in the world. We leave ourselves with the Critic, suppressing our spontaneity, our creativity.

To grow our own internal Divine Nurturer, we must believe there is an internal light within us that will never go out and that our healing is about making that light shine brightly. We have to be willing to love ourselves, caring about *all* of ourselves, as is evident by increasing our positive behaviors, not by decreasing our negative ones.

The job of the Nurturer is to meet the needs of the Divine Child in the present moment through compassion, knowledge, and creativity. There is a physical sensation of the Nurturer within your body. The presence of both a nurturing voice and a loving emotion enables you to nurture yourself first and then others.

When someone makes a loving statement to us out of a heartfelt sense of loving and caring (for example, "I'm glad to spend time with you," "You're magnificent," or "I am inspired by your ideas"), we are hearing that person's Nurturer. Later, when we remember these loving statements and hear them in our minds, we experience our personal Nurturer, even though at the beginning, it may use the tone of voice and words of another person.

The loving is what heals, not the reviewing of past pain. A review takes place in the Mentor; love emanates from the Nurturer. The Nurturer increases only through use, and the Critic can get smaller only with less exercise. One cannot happen without the other. It takes discipline, practice, and assistance from the Mentor to achieve this delicate balance. Learning to handle energy that is more positive can improve our relationships, health, and success.

Occasionally, I hear people say, "I'm so nurturing to other people that I must have a very big Nurturer." Unfortunately, the opposite is true. However, if we're overly nurturing of others, we have most likely failed to nurture our internal selves. When we nurture from something other than our own abundance, we begin to project our depletion on others, and we try to give to them what we need for ourselves. No one is satisfied in this process.

Some writers describe neurotic nurturing as codependent behavior produced by a sense of over-responsibility, the ability to move but not express on one's own behalf. Honest giving requires an internal process of receiving as well as giving so we can give from our abundance rather than from a need to receive something in return. Our receiving until we flow over occurs before our spilling out in giving. We can truly give to others only when we have given sufficiently and abundantly to ourselves. "Love thy neighbor as [you love] thyself" (Mark 12:31), not the other way around. In other words, only to the degree that we love ourselves can we truly love someone else.

No real love is exchanged when our reaching out to receive nurturing is misdirected, and instead of getting, we give something we don't have. We create counterfeit caring, fake love—empty words with no value. We create a deficit in ourselves and cheat the other person as well. No one feels satisfied. We spend energy for naught. This neurotic behavior is equivalent to child abuse, and the abused child is in you; you're the Wounded Child, starving for affection and care. In this process, the in-between space—God, Spirit, or heart—isn't honestly present. An illusion is created. Keep in mind that the Critic can imitate a loving person to manipulate others to get what it wants. Don't be fooled. Real love has an expansive feeling and doesn't confuse or restrict the physical body. Again, true giving comes from abundance. The abundance of the heart makes gratefulness, and gratefulness of the heart then makes happiness. We intrinsically find happiness in what is, not in what is phony.

The kind of childhood we had may have left us with a very limited ability to take in and really benefit from positive communication. We are all aware of the time it takes to get our bodies in shape through diet and exercise. We need just as much time to get our mental parts working at peak performance. Recognizing those nurturing statements others make is a place to start. Be patient and faithful to the process, and your inner Nurturer will come.

The Nurturer is composed of several of the traditional archetypes found in Caroline Myss's online library article, "A Gallery of Archetypes—Teacher, Advocate, Mediator, Wizard, and Good Mother." The Teacher instructs and communicates knowledge, skill, and wisdom to students. An Advocate comes to the defense of others through kind actions. The Mediator empathizes with all parties, using patience and insight to smooth or untie the tension knots of conflict. A Wizard uses supernatural powers (love is a supernatural power). The Good Mother possesses the infinite capacity to love and forgive her children and put them before her. All these gifts are part of our growing Nurturer.

In addition, included in our Nurturer are the characteristics of Jesus (as described in the first six books of the New Testament), who has served through centuries as a guide for loving behaviors. His characteristics include being unconditionally loving, nonjudgmental, forgiving, intuitive, protective, instructive, accepting, creative, and purposeful. Yes, the Nurturer unconditionally loves (has an open heart) even toward the Critic, because that is the only thing a Nurturer can do.

Fear and anger, emotions of the Wounded Child, are alerting mechanisms, whereas, love is letting go of fear, (Jampolsky). Love is an impulse to reach out with an open hand, an emotion and a behavior that belongs to the Nurturer. God is love (1 John 4:16). The deepest internal nurturing you can have gives love through guidance, common sense, intuition, and wise decisions; and with this Nurturer, the Child in you can say with confidence, "He [Nurturer] who is in me is greater than he[Critic] who is in the world" (1 John 4:4).

A fully developed Nurturer begins to heal the Wounded Child by listening to, acknowledging, and accepting the child's feelings. The Nurturer treats the Child with respect and acceptance. As the Child trusts the Nurturer to be ever present, a sense of receiving the love he or she has always wanted develops. The Wounded Child regresses in age from six to infinity, revealing each age's pain waiting for love. The Nurturer validates as real the unresolved pain or grief of the Wounded Child; the Child cannot grieve alone. The Nurturer must help resolve the feelings involved with grief, such as anger, depression, hurt, remorse, sadness, and loneliness. The Nurturer gives specific-to-the-point praise, is honest, and uses *I* messages more than *you* messages (for example, "I love you. I like you the way you are. I want you to be happy."). The Nurturer involves the creativity of the inner Child in problem solving and decision making relative to the Child's own needs and is respectful toward the inner Child's feelings, needs, wants, suggestions, and wisdom.

The Nurturer meets all the Child's hidden needs (wounds) at each age with Divine compassion (unconditional love). As the Child heals, he or she becomes younger, revealing stored pain at age five, then four, and so on until it reaches infinity. The wounds of the Child become fewer and fewer as the Child surrenders to the Divinity of the Nurturer's love. While ministering to the Child's internal needs, the Nurturer becomes larger and larger until it too reaches infinity—Christlike; it loves more, accepts more, and heals more of the Child's pain as the Child regresses to join the Nurturer as one in infinity.

The Wounded Child, healed to the point of infinity, becomes the Divine Child and surrenders to the infinite Divine

Nurturer. From the infinite, the Divine Nurturer and the Divine Child manifest as our Spiritual self. We are real to everyone. The conceptual distance between the *I* and *Me*, between *You* and *Yourself*, no longer exists. Your Spiritual self has no need for separation, no need to judge. No parts are lost; all are saved from the Critic.

When we express caring or gratitude to others and to ourselves, we need to be specific and say more than "That's good." Describe what is good. Give praise for actions, thinking, and being: "Good use of your time" (action), "Great idea" (thinking), "I enjoyed you today" (being), "I think you're so efficient" (action), "What a nice thing to say to someone" (action), "Good use of your imagination" (thinking), and "I like having you around" (being).

Don't be discouraged if during the first time you stop to listen to your internal Nurturer you hear only the voice of the Critic saying things like, "You can't do this" or "Oh, you don't need to change anything." Kindly—body posture relaxed, loving emotion, and pleasant tone of voice, compassionate—tell the Critic, "Stop and take a vacation." (Remember, the Critic shrinks with lack of use, so turn it off with a body change—a release of tension, and kind words: "Stop," "Take a vacation" or "Thanks but no thanks.")

The self-Nurturer matures through intention, attention, and exercise, lots of exercise. By using our free will, we make a conscious choice to grow our own Nurturer by choosing to be internally responsible. Once the use of the Nurturer is habitual, it holds all the internal power—light over darkness, good over evil, love over fear. "Jesus answered and said unto him, Get thee behind me Satan: for it is written Thou shall worship the Lord your God and Him only shall you serve" *(*Luke 4:8).

Exercise 11: A Loving Voice with Loving Words

Step 1: We communicate nurturing through our word choice, tone of voice, and body movement. Take some time now to make a list of past nurturing remarks that come to mind easily, such as "I really love you," "I'm very glad to be with you!", or "I feel good spending time with you." Make your list as extensive as your memory will allow. List only the ones you can recall. Be specific with anatomical parts; don't just use "back" or "front."

Personal Loving Remarks

Step 2: If you have difficulty or your list is short, go someplace where there are people with children—the zoo, grocery store, or park—and listen for nurturing statements parents make to their children. Write them down. Get back to a quiet place with yourself. Without looking at the list of statements you collected while listening to others, see how many you can now recall inside your mind. If you can recall only a few, take time to memorize them and store them in the Mentor. Then recall these statements and recreate them with the same vocal tones and body expressions as the person had when you first heard them. Express them from your Nurturer. Next, add them to your own nurturing list. This takes some time. Practice these statements until they become automatic remarks you say to yourself.

Step 3:

A. Continue with this until you can see the change in a mirror and can recognize the change in your voice and body. With the repeated remarks, your body and voice will feel smooth, kind, and relaxed. (Pretend you're an actor in a play again to help keep your Critic turned off.) Continue until your own internal nurturing list is as readily available and long as your critical list.

B. When you achieve these two steps, repeat your favorite statements in your nurturing voice. Notice how you feel in your body and how you feel emotionally. Until all of those outwardly directed nurturing statements are turned inward so your own Wounded Child's ears can hear them, the loving compartment inside you is yet to mature. Be persistent in adding to every compliment you give to someone a silent "and so am I." What eventually happens inside you will so surprise you.

Note: Practice this activity for several days or more before proceeding to Exercise 12.

Exercise 12: Create the Body and Voice of the Nurturer

The first step begins with paying attention to the nurturing words in your mind and then progresses to your body sensation as you think about these words. Last is your tone of voice when giving expression to each word—first thought, next body, then voice. In Step 5 the awareness process is somewhat reversed—body sensations first, thoughts second, and finally tone of voice. Our bodies know who is speaking subliminally before we have conscious thought. When we awake in a bad mood, our Critic has slipped in right before we're fully awake. Heightened awareness of our body, thoughts, and voice gives us power over how we choose to be as humans.

Step 1: Now choose one of the remarks from your completed Personal Loving Remarks list. Say it aloud, finding the appropriate voice and body position that fits the tone of voice for this remark. Speak calmly; embody your remark with your posture and facial expression. Become this nurturing character.

Step 2: As you hear yourself say these positive, loving words, you may notice your body soften in all the places where it is usually tense. Allow these body parts to soften more, to relax even more as you turn up the volume and listen inside your mind to your Nurturer.

Step 3: Hug a pillow; repeat your top-two favorite nurturing statements aloud as though you were saying them to a very young part of yourself. (This young part of you may cry with relief after waiting so long for someone to notice and care.) Remember, heart energy never runs out, and we can send it through our thoughts.

Step 4: Notice how you feel in your body and how you feel emotionally. Make a note of these in your Personal Loving Remarks list. Practice until you're aware of your nurturing body, even when words aren't present. It's imperative that you actually experience this process in your body rather than merely read about it.

Step 5: Reverse the process by focusing on your body first. Allow your body tension to relax, to let go. Notice the sensations in your body and your feelings. Now turn up the volume on your mental dialogue so you can hear what is being said when you aren't paying attention or don't hear it.

Step 6: Now, listen carefully to your nurturing words of the nurturing voice in your mind and notice the accompanying overt body posture. With increased listening awareness, you will be able to push the ON button by simply creating ease in your body. (When you have tension, your Critic is at work. Run it off by relaxing, by releasing tension.) A creative, descriptive summary of this process follows in the excerpt from Margery Williams's classic tale, *The Velveteen Rabbit*.

And then, a strange thing happened. For where the (little rabbit's) tear had fallen, a flower grew out of the ground, a mysterious flower, not at all like any that grew in the garden. It had slender green leaves the color of emeralds, and in the centre of the leaves a blossom like a golden cup. It was so beautiful that the little Rabbit forgot to cry, and just lay there watching it. And presently the blossom opened, and out of it, there stepped a fairy. She was quite the loveliest fairy in the whole world. Her dress was of pearl and dewdrops, and there were flowers round her neck and in her hair, and her face was like the most perfect flower of all. And she came close to the little Rabbit and gathered him up in her arms and kissed him on his velveteen nose that was all damp from crying.

"Little Rabbit," she said, "don't you know who I am?"

The Rabbit looked up at her, and it seemed to him that he had seen her face before, but he couldn't think where.

"I am the nursery magic Fairy," she said, "I take care of all the playthings that the children have loved. When they are old and worn out and the children don't need them anymore, then I come and take them away with me and turn them into Real."

Our life purpose is to grow our own "fairy," an internal mother, a Divine Nurturer. When our Nurturer becomes Divine, large enough to embrace all the characteristics of Christ, it will have grown beyond all physical limits into infinity; it becomes the keeper of our internal light.

We look for people to trust who will not take advantage of us when we're emotionally vulnerable—who will not attack, correct or make fun. We're also looking for those who will consistently support our excitement, our creativity in the moment, much like mothers who put our scribbled pictures on their refrigerators with praise. We allow ourselves to love these kinds of people because we trust them to protect, support, and join us at times that increase our joy.

Trust develops over time and through experience with the other person through time and experience. Trust isn't the tingling feeling you may have when you first meet someone. Those tingles may be the magnetism of each of your dysfunctions. At times, it simply means the other person is able to take down his or her physical or mental boundary and be available in the moment. At other times, it may appear that the person is open all the time. Keep in mind, when there is no boundary to push against, that the real person hasn't yet shown up—there are only smoke and mirrors. You will know whether there is realness through time and experience with this person.

Take the time to experience your younger self so trust can develop in your ability to self-nurture and self-support. Be worthy of your own trust. Discern your Critic in disguise as your inner Child or your Nurturer. Check the Nurturer's characteristic references at the beginning of this section. Be consistent with honesty and caring for yourself so trust can develop from within and then manifest in all your relations. A contented inner Child creates a happier adult. Remember, heart energy never runs out, and we can send it through our thoughts.

To create a different world, we must first create it within ourselves through our thinking. Then, through our actions, we give ourselves the love that is missing internally so it can manifest in the present in our external world. A loving, intimate relationship between our Divine Nurturer and Divine Child will provide a ground for a loving intimate relationship with someone else in our life.

Intimacy: I see into me. What would someone else see if he or she could see into you? Would he or she see an inadequate Nurturer, a guilty hurt Child, a confused mental self, enslaved by your Critic and following the will of others, resulting in no Spiritual self to share? I hope he or she would find you as your emotionally mature self—a mental body organized around free will and a Spiritual self that is larger than your physical form, sharing with others as a unified Nurturer, a loved creative Child, and an attentive Mentor united through your Spirituality.

Go for the gold. Create the best for you and the world. Jesus said, "God is love" (1 John 4:8) and "Where two or three are gathered in my name [love] there am I in the midst of them" (Matt. 18:20). When love is the intent and the expression between your Divine Nurturer and your Divine Child, you will experience the infinite.

Spontaneity is most creative and useful within a structure; inspiration can flow only if there is a channel for it. We see this truth even in schoolchildren at recess. If the playground has no fence, the children will play close to the building. However, when there's a fence, they play right out to the limit of the school grounds next to the fence.

We can now have a new structure within ourselves, a means of establishing and keeping alive the ongoing relationship with our inner Child, out of which our new life develops. Eventually our conflicts are resolved, revealing our spiritual presence.

Even though we understand (Mentor) all our personal past history and see the forces at work in ourselves that have shaped our lives, this by itself will not heal us. We must resist inertia and do something more to reconcile and integrate the archetypes of our unconscious with our conscious to alter our destructive inner situation (Critic) and bring new life (Divine Child).

We must give up the life blueprint, handed down through our family dynamics and sculptured within our minds, for a new more loving form. Our free will, the power to choose, is the most powerful thing we have. It is so powerful that even God won't interfere with it. We must mobilize this free will and choose faithfulness to act on our own behalf through our Christlike Nurturer. We must find and keep our hearts open. Although we're never alone, only each of us alone can do it.

STEP 5

DIVINE CHILD

The Self to Love

Verily, I say unto you, whosoever shall not receive the kingdom of God as a little child, shall in no way enter therein. —Luke 18:17

Except ye be converted, and become as little children, ye shall not enter into the kingdom of heaven.

—Matt. 18:3

TABLE 4: THE DIVINE CHILD

Spiritual Correlation
• Soul, child of God, spiritual self

Mental Construct
• Creative ideas, emotions, simple wisdom, truth
• Innocence, life purpose, inner Child, health, beauty
• Kindness, dignity, respect, peace

Physical Manifestation
• Pleasurable creations, playing, sharing, acts of love

The Divine Child's Characteristics

- Is ceaselessly creative
- Finds a sense of value present in everything
- Is spontaneous
- Is the source of all basic emotions
- Is eternally connected to the nonphysical

ROOM 4

THE DIVINE CHILD

The Divine Child contains our Soul energy, our full potential, and our purpose in this life. To manifest this magnificent force, we must travel back from where we came, back through the gateway of childhood, embracing with love each of our childhood wounds and their emotions until we arrive at the opening between the Spiritual and physical world. There we are all we are meant to be. We find the key to entering this place in the mental process of using our free will to become as a little Child and to trust and surrender to our Nurturer, who in turn embraces each childhood's emotional wound. To reiterate Jesus' ancient wisdom, "Unless ye be converted [unless you change] and become as little children, you shall not enter the kingdom of heaven" (Matt. 18:3).

Our innocent, sanctified Divine Child, for whom the portal opens, ensures our entrance into the kingdom of heaven. The essential quality of our Divine Child is its ceaseless creativity. Even when we aren't aware of it, this creativity works in the innermost center of our being. It doesn't stop, even when we're sleeping; it manifests itself in our dreams. The Divine Child hungers for those experiences that enable creative living and wants to live and play. The Divine Child never expresses itself in the same way twice.

Life lived from this part of the self is primarily a free-flowing life. This kind of life is different from moment to moment, and we are different from each other. From the Divine Child, our lives become works of art, capable of making innovative responses to the many difficult, perplexing problems and situations life brings to us.

A life lived in support of the Divine Child has intensity. The Divine Child makes life melodious, delicious, colorful, and satisfying. Even when things go badly, the Divine Child can create a sense of the presence of something with immediate value. The Divine Child trusts and believes that in the end, "all things [in the universe] work together for the good to them that love God" (Romans 8:28). Consequently, the innocence of the Divine Child opens the gateway between the Spiritual and physical worlds.

The Divine Child archetype radiates pure innocence. It has a redemptive mission and hungers for those experiences that enable spontaneous creative living. For most of us, the simple idea of continually living in Divine Innocence is daunting; hence, we have difficulty identifying with the Divine Child archetype within ourselves. In the beginning of life, we were there, and we can embrace that place in ourselves again. Think about it ... Mistrust (innocence lost) dissolves into forgiveness, into believing, into surrendering, into trusting, and back into innocence and love.

Some of us have experienced horrendous events in our younger lives, such as physical abuse, incest, neglect, and abandonment. We can congratulate ourselves for our survival skills. They saved our lives. We survived to be here now. However, no matter how bad the outer circumstances of life are, they cannot completely cut us off from our Divine Child.

Often we believe our pain and suffering are the fault of someone else rather than the inevitability of being human. Whatever the justification is for what has happened to us, it serves no purpose to reprimand ourselves into a victim state through hindsight or to expect more from ourselves than we can deliver in the moment. When doing so, we deny our inner Child entrance into the kingdom. We have yet to develop, to integrate our Nurturer as the guardian of our inner Child (in Christian ideology, Christ as our internal Savior), and in so doing we separate ourselves from Love (God).

Settling for survival isn't enough. Anger and blame haunt our images from the past and hurt others and ourselves in the present. Discontent fills our internal spaces. No matter how hard we try to change, our subconscious programs continue to run.

The neurological processing ability of our subconscious mind is more than a million times more powerful than the conscious mind (Lipton). By age six, we automatically operate with old programming in a rapidly changing world (not a good idea). We are completely unaware that our subconscious mind automatically, without control or interference, makes our daily decisions based on our perceptions acquired from others before the age of six—an age when imagination and reality are confused.

When we pay attention to our inner process, we will be surprised to discover the unusual belief system of the Child stored in the first six years of the Mentor.

I remember that on one occasion I stopped at a local gas station on a Sunday afternoon to purchase gas. I opened my tank, inserted the nozzle, and waited for the attendant inside to turn on the pump. I assumed another customer inside had distracted him.

As I waited, I noticed by the outside door a stack of Cokes with a sale price I couldn't resist. I picked up a twelve-pack and put it in my car, intending to pay for it when I went inside to pay for the gas. I redirected my attention to pumping the gas only to discover the pump was still not on. I now had been waiting for about fifteen minutes, daydreaming a little along the way.

I returned to the present, aware of the time, and decided I had waited long enough. A little agitated (my Critic), I went inside to ask the attendant to turn on the pump. He responded, "Oh, we are out of gas and won't have any until tomorrow." I returned to my car in a daze. "Gas stations are simply not supposed to run out of gas" (Critic).

As I continued driving down the street, I remembered I hadn't paid for the Cokes (Mentor). My Critic grabbed that thought and began calling me a thief. My Nurturer returned with an authoritative "Stop." My Child responded from a child's understanding of a belief that it and the Critic had both heard from my Mentor while I was daydreaming, "Time is money [a slogan on a clock I owned], and you waited a long time, so you don't have to pay for them. And besides we could buy something else with that money."

I was now aware that my Critic had used this same statement from the early years of my Mentor, "Time is Money," to create my aggravation about waiting and a sense of lack in my Child part. My Nurturer and Mentor put their heads together to understand the intent in the Child's response and to determine the best way to instruct the Child while maintaining love and integrity in the system of self.

My Nurturer asked, "What would you buy instead of paying for gas?"

"Ice cream," replied the Child.

Now was the time to give instruction, new information to the Child. "We have enough money to pay for gas, get the Cokes, *and* buy ice cream. If we don't pay for the Cokes, we won't be an honest person, and being honest makes us feel good. We can pay for the Cokes on the way back and get ice cream now. Would you like to get ice cream now?"

With an affirmative response from the Child, my Nurturer enlisted the help of the Mentor in remembering to stop on the way back and pay for the Cokes. We all went for ice cream.

By the time I started home, the Cokes in the backseat had completely slipped my mind, but not the Child or Mentor's. About a block from the gas station, I heard a voice inside say, *Remember to pay for the Cokes.* I stopped and paid the man, explaining what had happened. He went into an obvious trance, silently looking first at the money, then at me, and then back at the money. Returning to the car, I heard a little inner voice. *You were right; I do feel good when I'm honest.* I could even see her smiling.

A childhood wound is anchored in childhood beliefs stored in the beginning of the Mentor's collected information (life before six), and it fuels the childish Critic and the role-playing of a pretend Nurturer often seen in adults. As children, these adults often had an alcoholic or disabled parent or an elderly family member as a caretaker. We can never predict how this Wounded Child will act because it draws on the creativity of the Divine Child.

As children, we heard, "Grow up. Be a big boy or girl. Don't act like a baby." We try. We lock our feelings, our creativity, and our needs in the closet; and lose the key. (The truth is, we do the best we can in any given moment to survive in the world, as we perceive it.) This Child now bangs on the door, creating a headache or some other illness in an attempt to get our attention. Still, we look the other way and refuse to listen or feel. We turn up the radio or the television, take two aspirin, or start the cocktail hour earlier. We hurry or stay busy or talk too loud or too much so as not to hear the cries and wants of our inner Child. We project our gifts onto other people and admire or reject them.

Our Wounded Child, in need of healing, casts a shadow over our Divine Child. The Wounded Child resists love while displaying blame and self-pity. These wounded and fragmented parts hold a set of fixed beliefs, fears, and feelings—patterns of moving, thinking, and relating as a representation of old unmet needs. By the time we reach maturity, our natural relationship with our unique personality is lost. We have walled in our Wounded Child, cutting ourselves off from our Divine Child. This wall of fear and pain separates us from the innermost core of our individuality; the creative energy of the Divine Child is stifled and consequently restricts our Spiritual selves, our Souls.

We lost our connection to the fullness of our creative power through the way we had to live to survive in an imperfect world. We did this by creating our Critic. We continue to overexercise the Critic while doing nothing to develop our Nurturer. We continue to do so by failing to use our free will, conscious process of choice (Myss), to choose love over fear and criticism. When we refuse or restrict our Divine Child's expression, the internal pressure to create can manifest as health issues. The spontaneity and creativity of the Divine Child cannot freely flow into our daily lives because of our wall of body armor and frozen perceptions.

Our childhood wounds disconnect us from our essential integrity and health. Psychoanalyst Wilhelm Reich theorized that the continual blocking of expression of primary needs results in a chronic contraction of the musculature or body armor—the expression of the personality in the way the body moves. Rarely are we without some emotion, and with every emotion, there is a muscular response. We all have unexpressed emotions—feelings not allowed to surface, hidden in our muscles.

Locked-in emotions can give us high blood pressure, headaches, ulcers, irregular heartbeats, and much more. They can often lead to premature physical handicaps or even death. Our frozen body parts require energy to hold our emotions in place. When those emotions are released, better health, vitality, and quality of life result. Bodywork, especially massage and unstructured dance, confronts the emotional wounds where they are stored, in our bodies. We are always bodies in motion.

We cannot contain our inner Child in our conceptual formulations or turn it into an object as so many of the previous books on the market urge us to do. Contrary to these earlier writers, the inner Child never grows up, nor is it allowed to die.

If we try to control it, it will elude us. If we try to predict how it will act, it will act in an unpredictable manner. It will contradict our expectations and leave us when we try to harness it to goals of adult personal power.

However, we can decide to structure our thoughts in an organized fashion, and with consistent repetition there lie new pathways in our subconscious minds—patterns of acceptance, trust, love, and creativity. We become more skilled at creating that sought-after intimacy than our former caregivers did. We owe it to ourselves to create this kind of internal environment, the one we wanted when we were a child.

Our Mentor, Nurturer, and Child become our new internal family, and together they create the love and intimacy for which we longed. In turn, our actions mirror our thoughts and become new habits that fall into the background of our thinking, our subconscious. They act as our new automatic operating program.

One by one each wound must heal so we can open the door to our Divine Child. As the Nurturer accepts and heals the pain of each wound, the Wounded Child, in turn, moves into forgiveness and acceptance of Divine Love. The stagnant, energy-creating pain disappears, leaving in its place access to the gifts now integrated into all parts of our being. Then the magic happens. Our world, as we once saw it, changes. We are healthier, happier, and kinder; and our no thinking response is love.

Caroline Myss provides an extensive explanation of the characteristics and development of numerous archetypes, some of which represent our wounding process. Here I offer only the names and very brief definitions of four of her child archetypes.

The (1) "Orphan Child" holds onto the fear of surviving alone in the world, (2) the "Eternal Child" lacks a foundation for adulthood, (3) the "Dependent Child" focuses on his or her own needs over others, and (4) the "Innocent/Magical Child" believes that everything is possible (*A Gallery of Archetypes*, 2010, Myss).

Because the "Orphan Child" dynamics include pride in survival accomplishments, this Child can be very resistant to giving up its wound. Without the wound to motivate survival, the prideful sense of success that fuels self-righteous anger has no reason to exist. In such a situation, the Nurturer draws from the informed observing Mentor to teach the Child new family values as well as how to play and when to accept help, embrace union, and trust in others through group interaction in the external environment and then through internal relating between Nurturer and Child. (The Mentor may need to acquire this information from interacting in a therapy group.)

The "Eternal Child" archetype is unable to embrace the responsibilities of adulthood appropriately—this is the Peter Pan effect. The Mentor contains Peter-Pan-type qualities and needs to grow in wisdom. This developmental gap can occur in a normally intelligent child if he or she isn't exposed to standard intelligence starting at age two. If you find yourself in the Peter Pan effect, grow your internal Mentor by participating in a local mentorship program. Learn and understand independent adult responsibilities and behaviors. Once these are learned, the Nurturer assists the Child in executing the actions indicated by each responsibility the Mentor has recorded.

The "Dependent Child" has enormous unmet needs that compete to be met. Maslow's hierarchy of needs, stored in the Mentor, offers categories for sorting needs. The Nurturer discerns which need takes priority and finds a way to meet the selected need while most importantly teaching the child to savor satisfaction through body sensations in the present moment.

The "Magical Child", with the power of imagination, believes that moving in one's on behalf isn't necessary. The child's sense of powerlessness is managed through fantasy rather than through creative action. In healing the Magical Child, the mature Nurturer teaches the Child the difference between fantasy creativity and intent creativity. For example, young, small-framed boys, while never making the football team, often continue to dream of being a famous football star. In reality, the odds are against them; they most likely will remain physically lacking in traits necessary to meet the team's needs.

For most of us, external nurturers, such as parents, grandparents, club leaders, and teachers, anchor the Magical Child's dream in reality rather than encouraging it with "anything is possible" (a Mentor statement the Critic uses to keep the child stuck in an illusion). Instead, the Nurturer teaches and encourages the child with, "It never hurts to dream big. Anything is possible within the facts upon which a dream is built. Given the anatomical facts, plus your love of football (child's dream) and desire to earn large sums of money (security and stimulation-seeking fulfillment), there are many other possibilities—owning a team, sports broadcasting, coaching, and so forth."

The Nurturer teaches the child that action motivated by imagination produces a tangible reward (what, when, where, and how). The released energy the Magical Child previously used in fantasizing reverts to the Divine Child for creative imagining and motivates the physical body into dream-manifesting actions. The Mentor provides the facts, the Nurturer gives the wisdom for using the facts, and the Divine Child provides the creative force.

With concerted effort and practice, we can make Myss' "conscious process of choice" part of our subconscious pattern regardless of which Child shows up. By choosing to pay attention to our body's sensations moment by moment, by using our free will to choose how we think, and by examining our relationships as they reflect our internal success, we decide, like Eugene, Neil Simon's *Broadway Bound* character, "not to be most people."

Henceforth, we shall refer to all the aforementioned Child archetypes as a collective internal wound and reference all of them as the Wounded Child. The Nurturer discerns and identifies the wound as each Child presents itself and then meets that Child's need in the moment.

To summarize: In the present moment, our internal Mentor presents us with facts, and our openhearted inner Nurturer surrenders to the Child's need with total acceptance. It uses the (1) facts, (2) perceived need of the Child, and (3) the Child's imagination to mediate a harmonious solution, goal, or dream for the Child. No part gives up, compromises, or is talked into anything. The outcome must be pleasing, acceptable, and congruent with the Mentor, Nurturer, and Child. The Nurturer checks to be sure whether the Child is satisfied with the outcome. The Child's "yes" or silence ends the gestalt process;

the Child has the final expression of satisfaction. All are settled in you—peace.

A very religious neighbor of mine, where I previously lived, decided that sharing the idea of the tooth fairy and Santa Claus with her child was lying. She would have no part of it in their home. This child held a very important place in her heart. Both parents agreed to tell their very young daughter that there was no Santa or tooth fairy. However, by the time she was four years old, she would say, "I know, Mom, but let's just pretend. This is what I want Santa to bring me." And when other children asked what she got for Christmas, she would reply, "Santa brought me this."

Even though her parents were teaching her to reject these concepts, the other children she played with believed in them with all their hearts. Her entire extended environment said Santa *did* exist. To be like others her age, she had to do something with the Santa archetype. Her conflict? "I want to be like other kids, and my mom wants me to think Santa isn't real." She very cleverly resolved her conflict with one word: *pretend.*

Her parents wrapped her presents just as they did each other's; the tag said, "From Mamma and Daddy." And when she opened her presents, she said, "Look what Santa brought me." When they confronted her again, she replied, "I'm only pretending." (Obviously that's something the parents couldn't do.) They let her comments pass so as not to spoil the day with conflict. That is how we select our personal archetypes. I hope she will integrate her archetypal Santa and play Santa with her own children. If not, this is likely to remain a childhood wound, manifesting from her subconscious in ways outside her awareness.

We too can pretend. Whether we believe in or just imagine the symbols to understand the words revealing the archetypes of Christianity all around us, we must integrate them or remain in conflict with our own being and culture. The archetypes are beyond our concept of accepting or rejecting them, because they are in our language and culture. Denied or accepted, they are part of our existence.

I often tell teenagers to "just make it up" instead of saying "I don't know" when asked about their beliefs. They then present me with amazing theories and ideas. Do they lie? Of course not. They let the words "make it up" act as a key to get them past their own resistance, fears, and judgments. The teens allow their storehouse of creativity and knowledge about themselves to come forth from their subconscious.

The subconscious, the playground of the inner Child, doesn't lie. Although the technique of active imagination brings the image and voice of the unconscious into focus, we need to do more than just passively watch. We need to act. An alert and participating Nurturer can create an intense symbiotic tie to the Wounded Child while maintaining the ability to tolerate separation and aloneness.

By meeting the unmet needs of your younger self, your Nurturer matures in love, growing into infinity. The Wounded Child, receiving love, regresses to the next painful age until there is no more walled in pain—the Child getting younger and younger and the Nurturer becoming gigantic until they join into one. From their oneness flows Divine Love—God's creative energy at work in us. It is always genuine.

When this process is in motion, the individual fills Spiritually, mentally, and then physically to the point of overflowing with love. Moreover, it is from this abundance, from this literal electrical sensation in the physical body, that we love others and bring peace to the world. The capacity for love comes from the universe and flows through our Nurturer and out to others.

Our Divine Nurturer and Divine Child merged into the Ultimate Spirit. The Wounded Child's acceptance of love offered through the Nurturer's embodiment of the characteristics of the archetypal Jesus, the Christ, results in a physical feeling as if one were escaping and leaving the physical boundaries of earth. The Divine Child is free from the physical burdens of life. From that experience, our painful memories heal. We become one with all of ourselves in the infinite, the eternal. Our memories no longer have an emotional hold on us. They are simply memories.

At age twelve, my sole purpose in life seemed to be to wash dishes and clean the kitchen. My mother cooked three meals daily. She used every pot in the kitchen to prepare food for six people. Often I dreaded coming home from school to a kitchen piled high with dishes. I became very good at kitchen duty while storing all my resentment in my body.

As an adult in my own kitchen, I wash everything as I go. My husband did not. I felt annoyed when I cleaned up behind him. Out of my awareness, my stuck inner Child was doing the dishes. After focusing my attention on my body and feeling my emotional tension, I discovered that I could simply make an internal adjustment in my body with an internal statement.

"You don't have to clean the kitchen. I will do it," said my Nurturer to my Wounded Child. "You can play." Peace replaced irritation as my nurturing part cleaned and my Child played in her daydreams, imagining all kinds of fun and interesting things for us to do later. Of course, my hands continued to be the ones doing the dishes, but my perspective changed. I saw the situation from adult eyes rather than from my twelve-year-old eyes. My perception of responsibility shifted from my Child self to my adult self. That small shift in perception satisfied the Child's need for help and made the task less arduous. My tense diaphragm relaxed its wall of tension, releasing my long-held-back tears. With shifts in perspective and my continual awareness of any tension in my body, I'm now able to breathe fully while relaxing my diaphragm. Remembering to breathe when placed in an overwhelming situation keeps me out of fear and in love.

The following phrases are examples of fixed childhood beliefs stored in the early years of the Mentor, the part that holds childhood beliefs, values, and facts.

- Every man for himself
- Adults keep children safe
- Treat everybody the same
- Girls are smart, and boys are strong
- My name is ...
- Everybody is equal
- There is always someone responsible
- You're always supposed to obey your parents
- Be nice and don't point out others' shortcomings
- You're supposed to like everybody
- Things are suppose to be fair

We introjected beliefs and childhood traumas that affect our self-image, and out of these wounds, we project the conflict and negative feelings onto other people. By becoming aware of these traumas and working consciously through them, we open and reenergize valuable and creative forces in the psyche, which implodes around the original trauma, tying up our life energy. These wounds are healed through love emanating from the infinite source, flowing through the created Nurturer (modeled after Jesus), clearing the path for our Divine Child (Child of God).

The Critic (Rules and demoralizing statements)

- Go ahead and step on people to get what you want
- You deserve to be punished (guilt, guilt)
- So what if he breaks your toys? Everyone suffers at one time or another
- Go ahead
- Show her how strong you are and hit her
- Well, nobody loves you enough to be responsible for helping you
- You're always going to be a loser, so don't try

Child without a Nurturer (poor physical and emotional boundaries)

- I will have to help myself...no one cares
- I'm only good sometimes
- I can hide
- I can pretend to be grown up

Religious history reports that Satan (represented by our Critic) failed when he tried to control the Divine Child of God through the crucifixion of Jesus. In turn, the resurrection of the body of Jesus, the changing of his name to *Christ,* and the placing of him on the right-hand side of the throne of God serve to remind us of the ultimate authority of love/God and the love and respect due our own Divine Child. Clearly, the archetypal Satan continues to manifest through the Critic in an attempt to prevent our own Divine Child from taking its rightful position next to our Nurturer (Christ in us).

The recounting of Christian religious history has served many for over two thousand years as a model for living a Spiritual life. In this process of healing the mind, it matters not that you believe this really happened. What matters is what you do with these images. All are archetypes that help us believe in a mystical, Spiritual place. When these archetypes move out of our imagination and into our physical expressions of who we are, then we say they have integrated into parts of ourselves. They move through us in our thinking, and in turn our bodies express them as actions.

With traits of Jesus in us, we have the right to claim our authority through God as Jesus demonstrated with the statement, "Ye are from God, little children, and have overcome them [critical statements, Satan]; because greater is He [Christ, Holy Spirit, Nurturer] who is in you than he [Satan, Critic] who is in the world" (1 John 4:4).

In the vernacular of Christianity, our innocent and dependent inner Child (Wounded Child) accepts Jesus, the Christ (Nurturer), who takes all our (human) pain and suffering (body sensations, armor), and we (all the ages of our Wounded

Child) are forgiven of our sins (our humanness, our Critic) and filled with the Divine Spirit (our oneness with all creation).

Although multiple religions lay claim to this process, it isn't a club requiring membership: we don't have to pay dues to use the map. It is free to anyone who wants to use it. When we use it with consistency as a blueprint for our mental patterns, our expression of internal peace becomes a contribution to world peace.

Through the following exercise, you can establish a Spirit-to-Spirit connection between you and your young self so the two of you can freely and lovingly join each other at the level of Spirit. Although this is a very elementary spiritual act, it is an affirmation and an experience of a profound union; your Nurturer and your Child from the past (under age six) are present with each other. This arrangement begins to build the Child's trust in you and your personal integrity.

The idea of the exercise is to create a symbolic image of you now with your Child self. Create an image (in your imagination) of the two of you joined. This imagery can take any form that satisfies your sense of oneness. For example, you can picture both of you surrounded by Divine Light. You may picture yourself and your inner Child eating from the same plate or sharing the same glass. You may picture the two of you hugging, sitting, or walking together hand in hand (my favorite). You may choose to be more symbolic in your imagery and picture the two of you as two flowers in the same vase, two raindrops in the same puddle, or two rolling waves in the same sea. You may picture your younger self inside your skin. Use whatever image facilitates your choice to be present in the between realm—Spiritually one with this part of yourself. What is divine is never limited by what is physical.

Exercise 13: Spirit to Spirit

This process has four steps: (1) grounding, (2) directing, (3) connecting, and (4) closing. You might wish to read aloud and record this exercise or have someone read it to you while you stay in the process for the whole of the experience. (If you stop to read, you aren't providing continual presence for yourself.)

Step 1: Grounding, Centering in the Body

A. Begin by closing your eyes and focusing your attention on your breath, breathing in through your nose and out through your mouth. Notice the sensations your breath creates in your nose and throat and on your lips.

B. Breathe until your body, breath, and thoughts become as one and until you feel soft and blended.

C. Expand your chest with your breath as you relax your abdomen. Begin to count down ("ten, nine, eight ... two, one"), becoming more relaxed with each number, allowing your head to slowly drop to your chest and your jaw to drop.

D. Say your name quietly each time you exhale until you grow quiet. Your name becomes a mantra, a sound that has Spiritual power. This act distracts your mind so you can feel your Spiritual presence.

Step 2: Directing Attention

A. Once centered in your body (Step 1), you may direct your attention to your Divine Child. Direct your attention to the physical presence of your young self. Notice the appearance of yourself under the age of six. What is your younger self wearing? What is your younger self doing? Tease out every detail as though you were drawing a picture.

B. Look at the image lovingly and peacefully until you can say, "I am present to your Spirit."

C. Should you become distracted, simply return to directing your attention by focusing on this image of your young self.

Step 3: Connecting to Others

A. Envision or imagine the two of you physically present to each other and forming a bond. Imagine that both of you are standing and facing each other while smiling and holding hands.

B. Make a choice to create what you envision, to make the union of you and the other person a reality (an inner reality but nonetheless a reality). Choosing a result you want is a central experience of who you are. Spiritual presence with your Child of the past directly offers you the opportunity to unite your love and will, and to express the real you that you are.

Step 4: Bringing Closure

    A. Draw or arrange objects as a symbol of this union. This is an action step, proof to you of your sincerity.

    B. Pretend that your Child (six years old or younger) is holding your hand as you walk out the door. As you get in the car, ask him or her, "Do you want to sit in the front or the backseat?" This is another fun action step.

    C. Be sure to listen to the reply and act accordingly in your imagination.

We will assume at this point that you've acquired the skill set needed to accomplish the internal task of exploring the final room of the mind, representing your archetypal Child's thoughts and feelings. This skill set includes the following:

1. Breathe
2. Tense and relax my muscles
3. Use my right brain or left brain
4. Shift my perception
5. Limitlessly create in my imagination
6. Use good listening, parenting, and negotiating skills.

This list helps identify which areas are weak and likely to cause frustration with you and others. The weak areas may need strengthening before you complete the upcoming task. You can do this by modeling someone who has proved successful in a particular skill or by taking a class.

Sometimes the Mentor needs to hone good listening, parenting, and negotiating skills so the Nurturer will have some new information to draw on. Otherwise you will use the same parenting style your parents used, creating the same mistakes that developed your Critic in the first place. You will just be going in a circle, repeating the past.

Loving parents enhance positive feelings in their children by using the following behavioral guidelines. Your internal Nurturer can use these with your own inner Child. On a scale of one to ten, with ten being the best possibility, rate yourself in each of the following six innate skills. I am able to do the following:

1. Listen to, acknowledge, and accept the Child's feelings
2. Accept and treat the Child with respect as is
3. Give honest praise about something specific
4. Use *I* messages rather than *You* messages
5. Involve the Divine Child in decision making relative to Nurturer and Child
6. Respect the Child's feelings, needs, wants, suggestions, and wisdom.

In addition to needing love, every external and internal Child needs the following from a primary caregiver to develop into a functioning whole adult:

1. Understanding (being heard or listened to)
2. Stimulation (active engagement)
3. Recognition (positive attention, validation)

4. Security (boundaries, food, shelter)
5. Companionship (togetherness)
6. Information (instructions or teachings)
7. Freedom of imagination without judgment, shame, or criticism.

One or more of these areas represents our younger self's core wound, because none of us had perfect parents.

Exercise 14: Then and Now Parents

Take the time to recall, write, or trace the history of your painful life situations from earlier memories to the present. Note what you particularly remember. What are the sounds, images, feelings, smells, tastes, or touches? They will be different for each memory. Flush them out; note your age and the presence or absence of anyone else. Make a guess as to where in your body you hold each one of these emotional memories, for you do hold them in your body, not just in your mind—first Spirit, then mind, then body.

Step 1: On a separate sheet of paper, make a list of painful childhood memories. Use descriptive words rather than *good* or *bad*. Describe the type of parent you had and then the kind you needed. Begin at age six and work backward through age five, four, and finally three.

Step 2: Notice what is different between your actual childhood parent and your needed parent. This is what is missing and what your Nurturer must provide. The Nurturer is your new parent. It is no one else's responsibility; no other person in the world can do enough for you to heal your wounds. Jesus advocated that he could be the role model for your Nurturer. Accept that truth and love yourself.

Step 3: Choose two from the following list of primary needs that best fit your need as a Child and work at allowing your Nurturer to meet each need in your hurt Child from the past. Nurture in the way you need it done, not in the way Mamma or Daddy nurtured you. Get good at it! Make a commitment to yourself.

- Understanding (being heard or listened to)
- Stimulation (actively engaged)
- Recognition (positive attention, validation)
- Security (boundaries)
- Companionship (togetherness)
- Information (instructions or teachings)
- Freedom of imagination without judgment, shame, or criticism

Step 4: Now commune Spirit to Spirit with your younger self of less than six years old (see Exercise 13) and find the object of his or her desire. It may be different at each age and at different times when you do this exercise.

Repeating the above exercise with yourself will bring forth new information from your deepest self. As you do, your six-year-old will becomes younger and younger, even to the time before conception, until all that remains is your original self. As this happens over time, your Nurturer becomes larger, expanding into infinity. Infinity is where your Divine Child and your nurturing self are one—you are Spirit with all.

The Nurturer provides a safe environment for self-expression, the basic need of the Child. The hurt Child in us talks only to the Nurturer. Stop the dialogue between the Critic and the Child with a simple "Stop!" Use simple, concrete language.

- It's okay to be scared.
- I love and protect you.
- Take all the time you need to trust me to protect you.
- I'm patient.

Speak to your hurt Child much as you would to a child in the room with you. Bear in mind that this Child never grows up. It merely becomes integrated. Use your Nurturer's voice and body. What needs to happen is this: from your Nurturer's voice and body, say, "Stop" to your Critic so it will shrink from disuse. Continue from your Nurturer to instruct, solve problems, encourage, and love the Child. In turn, your Nurturer will, with practice, grow larger in love, healing your hurt Child and creating a correct inner balance. So learn some new parenting skills. Observe other parents with children. Read books or attend a class if you must. Many cities and schools have parenting centers that offer classes and make their suggested readings available. Become the best loving, guiding, teaching parent to yourself you can be.

Love with the style and accepting compassion of Jesus. Listen to understand, please, and provide resolutions. Be willing to walk in the shoes of your wounded younger self. Become as that little child, moving and expressing. Be as generous as Jesus, feeding the multitudes with five loaves and seven fishes. Expect the good you have in your heart to multiply.

Provide security through meeting your basic needs for food, shelter, and care. Set boundaries for your physical world: when to sleep, when to eat, the kind of friends who support your full Spiritual self. Set mental boundaries: what you will read and view, the type of language you will use and hear. Set Spiritual boundaries: time to be with yourself and nature, to enjoy beauty and peace, and to pray or meditate.

Provide companionship by setting aside time to commune with yourself and time with others. Teach and reassure your younger self that life can be better for both of you, that you have come to prepare the way for a happier, more fulfilling life. Allow freedom of imagination without judgment, shame, or criticism. Greet your young self with excitement and delight. Out of our imagination, we create life; and through this process, we claim everlasting life.

One of these primary needs, when not met, always underlies the most outrageous demand or want of the Child in you, as illustrated in the following story. If you find otherwise, it may be your Critic portrayed as your whining Dependent or Orphan Child. Our archetypal Satan, the master of disguise, is very clever and seeks to be in the limelight at any price. Rebuke it kindly by saying, "Stop. You aren't my child. Leave my presence."

Remember that

- this process requires the Critic to take a vacation; and
- the Child never takes care of the adult Nurturer. Never.

The following are two examples of how an unmet inner-Child need can manifest in our everyday adult lives.

Big Baby

When I watched Adam enter the room, I could envision an eighteen-month-old baby in diapers. Adam was short and stocky, a roly-poly kind of person everybody liked. Being a mental health provider, he was interested in self-discovery and personal growth, and I wondered how history had produced his body image. What baby need had gone unmet all these years in Adam? The big-baby image stuck.

On this occasion, Adam had made an appointment to resolve a personal problem. It seemed Adam was obsessed with buying a sailboat, a *big* sailboat! Since he lived next to a lake and saw people sailing every day, his desire wasn't altogether unreasonable. However, buying a boat threatened his financial security. He understood that bankruptcy, should he be able to secure a loan for such a purchase, would soon ensue because of his unstable income. Still he obsessed and felt less than joyful.

Fear of acting on his obsession had brought him in for help. Our Child self has a childlike perception, so it never needs ego-type things such as a big boat or car. Adult objects are never the answer for the Child. Still, we try to appease it with such unsatisfying things. Adam worked through the process of identifying the categories of his thinking to establish the authority of the Nurturer within himself. He asked the inner Child whether a toy boat to play with in the tub would be acceptable. The answer was, "Oh, no, not at all!" We explored further. "What would you get if you had a big sailboat?" The inner Child replied, "I could rock all the time." Bingo! The connection between the big-baby body type was clear. The Nurturer, with an adult perspective, created an alternative way for rocking. Because his inner Child trusted his Nurturer to have his best interests at heart and to keep promises, the suggestion to purchase a big rocking chair and place it on the porch looking out at the lake so he could rock every day for an hour pleased his inner Child.

The Nurturer stopped the Critic's comments of "You don't have time to just goof off. People will think you're lazy rocking away like that."

Follow-up revealed that Adam's obsessive thinking stopped after three weeks of rocking. By then rocking was a habit and something the adult Adam enjoyed as well, especially when he needed nurturing. You cannot lightly dismiss the needs of your inner Child by just going through the motions once or twice.

After about a year, Adam looked less like an overgrown baby. The baby needs had been satisfied. A little more of his inner Child had been reclaimed. He was more in touch with his Spirituality. Ask whatever you [Divine Child] wish, and I [Christ, Nurturer] shall do it for you [Divine Child]. "Ask, and it shall be given you, seek, and ye shall find; knock and it shall be opened unto you" (Matt 7:7-8)

Shoplifting

Another client was a shoplifter. She'd stolen expensive dresses and on one occasion had gone to jail for this behavior. Out of fear of going to jail again, she sought help. When she began to commune with her younger self, she discovered that her primary underlying need was to be seen, validated, and recognized. As a teenager, she'd wanted to be a model. Unfortunately, she didn't have the height, body type, or opportunity to fulfill her dream. She hadn't connected her shoplifting to this unmet need.

Through dialoguing, her Nurturer and younger self came up with a creative solution. She and her sister, a professional photographer, would go shopping and try on expensive dresses. Her sister would take her picture. Then she would have the pictures enlarged to poster size and framed as art. Eventually, she sold them in all sizes as insert images for a picture frame manufacturing company. Knowing that other people viewed her picture fulfilled her need for validation and ended her shoplifting behavior.

We all want things we cannot have at times. When this happens, we can change what we want through our creative imagination and deep dialogue to discover the underlying need that produces the want. We don't need a specific memory. A sensation or emotion will do.

Usually each mental part holds a different perspective on any given issue or idea. Fear mixed with excitement is your Child embracing a vision of the future. Reassure the Child and move forward. Fear with a sense of dread is your Critic scaring your Child. Protect the child and take a different path. Fear usually lies somewhere in the background. Shine the light on it. If it belongs to the Nurturer, then recheck the Nurturer's characteristics. It could be your Critic in disguise. If fear lies with the Child, then instruct and reassure it. (You're brainstorming with your Child, not manipulating it.) You want to discover shared interest, to work for a positive outcome, a mutual gain.

In 1950, Erik Erikson, a Freudian ego psychologist, expanded Freud's theory of five developmental stages into eight stages. The following are three of the stages prior to seven years old—when each stage unfolds, the issues addressed at each age, and the emerging character strength. These represent the time a particular need may have been denied. If your Wounded Child appears to you at one of these ages, then the Nurturer with this information from your Mentor can address the growth issue for that particular age.

- Zero to twenty-nine months (trust through consistency without mistrust)
- Twenty-nine months to three years (autonomy without shame or doubt, the emergence of determination, willpower)
- Three to seven years (initiative balanced with guilt, the emergence of purpose). Psychopaths are the only people who feel no guilt. Imagination plus initiative produces purpose.

The felt instability of the adult person is due to a missing brick in his or her basic developmental needs. It is the Nurturer's responsibility to travel back in time and meet these needs. Some affirmations for any of the above stages include the following: "I love you just the way you are," "I'm glad you're a girl/boy," "Take your time; I have all the time in the world to meet your needs," "I am here to comfort you," "I think you can do it," "I want you to choose," and "You're special to me."

The Child always gets what it wants and has the last word. Its wishes are unreasonable only from an adult perspective. This is where teamwork between the two produces an original thought—creativity at its best. Otherwise, you aren't finished, and you're abandoning your Child self, a valuable creative resource of energy.

When you begin to dialogue with your Child from the past, you may discover some of the signs of low self-esteem found in children. The following list will help in identifying these signs:

- whining, blaming others, constantly apologizing
- needing to win, cheating
- being perfectionistic
- exaggerated bragging, overpleasing, giving away personal items
- using attention-getting devices: clowning; being self-critical, withdrawn, or shy
- distrusting, overeating

Over the next few weeks, notice whether your imagined Child is pleased when you purchase something for fun or do something spontaneous and enjoyable. Never try to talk your Child into something it doesn't want. For example, your Child wants a twenty-five-cent sucker, but you think a two-dollar chocolate bar is bigger and therefore better, so you try to override your Child's wish by talking him or her into what you think is better. Perhaps one of your parents did this to you.

Time

All sense of time and space is altered when we evoke a relaxation response, a sense of an altered state of consciousness—a trancelike state similar to drifting off into space when traveling or praying. In a trancelike state, all past and future time is *now*. Reality, as our five senses perceive it, is placed in the background. We sink into ourselves at a different time and place, and connect with our five senses in the then and there. Now is the time of a surreal moment, an "aha." This frequently happens during a right-brain activity, a trance or meditative state, or a deep state of prayer.

The ancient Greeks used two words to describe time, *chronos* and *kairos*. *Chronos* represents chronological or sequential time. *Kairos* represents indeterminate time. Reality established through our five senses and discussed as clock or *chronos* time is represented as a horizontal line in Figure 11. When we speak of the past or future, measurable moments in our thinking, we use this kind of time, the time we measure based on the revolution of the earth around the sun.

Kairos time points to significant moments in our thinking process and is unrelated to clock time. Thoughts of desire live in *kairos* time when God acts, a supreme moment when all things are possible. In *kairos* time, we can see and hear from within rather than from our current environment. It is in these moments that we integrate our archetypes, have an epiphany, and contemplate existential nonreality, such as our experience of the Spiritual, the mystical, and the infinite. A vertical line in Figure 11 represents this kind of time.

Figure 11: The Crossroads of Time

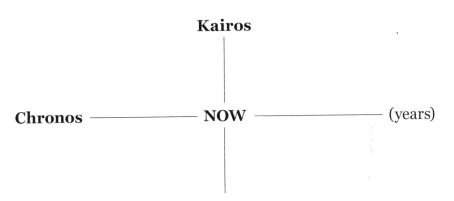

It is *kairos* time that allows us to visit our inner-life landscape and bring the past and future into the present for healing. Until they are healed, painful memories of the past or unrealistic dreams of the future influence the present moment of choice. Even though the past creates an epigenetic environment for the *now*, the past remains only an imagined event. How we respond to our memories at the time where *chronos* and *kairos* lines cross changes our future. "Be not ignorant of this one thing, that one day is with the Lord as a thousand years, and a thousand years as one day" (2 Peter 3:8). It is here, at this crossroad, that we transcend the boundaries of time, when we can be in a constant state of prayer while, at the same time, be in physical reality. Giving meaning to both brings order, and order precludes peace.

When a child begins to separate and leave the mother, he or she will choose an object, such as a baby blanket, to replace her presence. The blanket is a transitional object, an object that serves as a bridge between something we leave behind and something toward which we move. It represents an experience shared in both *chronos* and *kairos* time. We are in this transitional space when we pray or meditate; we place in the background our five physical senses relative to our environment to commune with Spirit. When we do this, we too often use a transitional object, such as a crystal, a polished stone, a prayer shawl, a rosary, or a cross to help shift us into a feeling or place of peace we want to experience again.

As we practice and become more comfortable with ourselves in this process, we can give up the actual object for an imagined transitional object. We may imagine the feel of the rock, the sound of a drum, the sight of the cross, or the sound or feel of our own breath. People who can make this shift quickly are usually very intuitive.

What are your transitional objects, and where are they located in your home? What bridge do they serve? Do they connect the past to the present, the physical to the Spiritual, the living to the dead?

Long-term memories of your Wounded Child living in *kairos* time need a trance state to produce change. Within this framework, *kairos* time allows both your young self and your present-age self to exist together in the same moment at the crossroads. You can travel back in chronological time (*chronos*) and save the Child in memory time (*kairos*) from the pain that it carries in your body now (chronos). It is here where you bring your wise, mature self's compassion and wisdom to heal the pain of your younger self and become one with all—a flower in full bloom.

Exercise 15: Counting Down through Time

Step 1: Read aloud with a slow rhythm and your most dreamy, calm voice and record the following:

"Get comfortable ... Close your eyes ... Release all tension ... Even now you can begin to count slowly backward from ten to one, allowing your sense of *chronos* time to drop into the background as you progress closer to the number one and enter *kronos* time. Now, counting down into yourself, ... (ten ... nine ...) you relax more (eight, seven ...), beginning to cross the threshold into *kronos* time. (six ... five ... four ...) In this state, recall a special, happy time in your life under six years old. (Pause five seconds.) Feeling your little hands ... and little feet, see what you saw ... (Pause five seconds.) Hear what you heard ... (Pause five seconds.) Feel what you felt ... (Pause five seconds.) Smell what you smelled ... (Pause five seconds.) and taste what you tasted ... (Pause ten seconds.) Now, slowly count yourself up, ... (four) becoming more aware of your body, ... (five) more aware of your breath ... (six ... seven), hearing the sounds around you ... (eight), opening your eyes ... (nine and ten), being fully present in *chronos* time. (Being in this moment with all five senses keeps us from simply watching it from an adult perception as a memory.)

Step 2: Play your recording and listen.

Only in this trancelike, meditative state can you really know the unmet needs and suppressed feelings in the body of your young self, which are restricting the body-felt excitement of you as an adult. In any other state, you're merely guessing, and this will not heal. Understanding doesn't heal. Being there, providing what is needed, does heal.

As a child, to survive in your family environment, you learned ways to protect yourself, such as withdrawal, desensitization, hallucinations, delusions, and flight. You used all these techniques to suppress your excitement, which pushed you toward getting your needs met. Our need to survive overshadows our need for a hug from a workaholic, alcoholic, or otherwise-involved parent, who might scream at us or reject us in some other way. We can live without a hug but not without shelter over our heads. Many people in a recovery program initially try to deny their addictive selves through these same survival strategies. They will own up (Mentor) to being an addict but will do nothing with the creative energy (Child) captured within. Shame and superiority, both of which the Critic created, must be overcome.

Expect your younger self to continue to employ one or more of these defenses with your adult self until you've gained its trust. These behaviors unnecessarily disrupt your ability to deal successfully with new situations. This is your neurosis. Your goal now is (1) to provide the safety needed to eliminate these beliefs in your younger self, (2) to provide what is needed, and (3) to release your creative energy locked in your muscles. This process, in turn, improves your contact with others. More of you is present. Remember, if you feel anxious when you are in this process, your anxiety is the dread of your own daring. It is fence-sitting between fear and excitement. Take responsibility. Get off the fence. Be afraid and address your fear (is it real or imagined) or be excited and progress.

Again, the first step begins with identifying your moment-by-moment mental and physical bodies. Who is talking in your mind? Your Mentor, Critic, Nurturer, or Child? Where is the tension or ease in your body? The second step is to choose to take on the characteristics of Christ, our role model, to manifest love. Displaying the characteristics of Christ is evident by the absence of body tension and your younger self trusting your consistency.

How free are you to pretend? Accept the challenge, take a moment, and recall the characteristics of the Nurturer:

- unconditionally loving
- non-judgmental
- peaceful
- intuitive
- forgiving
- accepting
- protective
- instructive

Now sense your younger self as he or she looks over your shoulder, watching you, as you pretend or imagine yourself putting on these characteristics, walking into the Spiritual body of the archetypal Christ. Hear the voice of this archetype as it speaks internally to your Wounded Child. Allow this Child part of you to accept (relax your body) the comfort your words bring. You're rescuing your Child from the Critic (doubt, resistance) and believing that the Child (you) deserve to be rescued and loved and to live forever in the kingdom of heaven in *chronos* and *kairos*. Your Divine Child, united with your Nurturer, becomes your Spiritual self. Just imagine it for a moment longer.

"You are from God, little children, and have overcome them [critical voices, Satan], because greater is he [Christ, Nurturer] that is in you [your whole self] than he [Critic, Satan] that is in the world" (1 John 4:4).

There is a profound difference in the atmosphere of a room when people are portraying their Critic versus their Nurturer. You may recall the sense of tension when you enter a room where people have just been arguing compared to the feeling you have in a place where people have been praying.

Developing a Nurturer in a group setting and securing a line of communication with the inner Child always affect those watching and listening. Some are lost in the content. They are moved emotionally as they imagine the Child component of the focus person to be their own inner Child. Others see the higher order of the experience and feel the Spiritual presence in the moment.

Example

On one occasion, I was working with a woman who grew up in another country. The group had gone through all the exercises of identifying the felt body sense and language of each of the four divisions of thought. Elizabeth began her individual work in the group of actually encountering her inner Child under age six. She spoke to her inner Child with all the correct learned skills of her Nurturer. However, the Child didn't respond, even in an altered state. I observed by her body language and effect that young Elizabeth couldn't hear or understand what the Nurturer was saying.

Elizabeth had grown up with a very strict, critical father who died when she was nine. Her mother soon married again and moved the family to the United States. Elizabeth didn't learn English until the age of eleven. She was at this time fifty-two years old and in a thirty-day hospital recovery program for addiction.

I simply asked her to speak from her Nurturer to her inner Child in the language the Child knew. Then I directed her to move to another chair and count in her native language, count herself down into the altered state of her Child, ... feeling her little hands ... and little feet ... and seeing what she saw ... and hearing what she'd heard when she was five.

In this state, as in any trance, the Mentor observes and calculates the information communicated through the images and feelings the Child presents. The Child is never asked to speak aloud, though sometimes it does if one is in a deep hypnotic state.

When Elizabeth came out of the trance state, she took a moment, stood up, and moved to her Mentor's body and voice; and then she reported in English the Child's experience. Moving to the Mentor before taking on the mental part and body position of the next role creates clear physical and vocal boundaries between all parts and aids in keeping the proper characteristics assigned to each designate room or part.

This was a new process for the group, so there was no guarantee that Elizabeth's Nurturer could negotiate the needs of the Child with her current life. Elizabeth spoke from the Nurturer in her native language, which no one present could understand. How could we tell whether she was using her Nurturer or judging from the Critic? We observed her body and voice, changes in effect and tone.

This time the group couldn't get lost in the content of the words. They had to watch for the clues of success—gentleness in the Nurturer's voice, release of body tension and effect change in both the Nurturer and the Child. The atmospheric change in the room and the presence of peace and serenity as Elizabeth and her younger self communicated completely surprised and awed all of us.

Then Elizabeth went one step further. She became her Child self at eleven and spoke in English to her imagined deceased father as though he were the Nurturer; she gave him a gift of all the Nurturer characteristics she'd used with herself earlier. She allowed him (through her belief system) to leave behind (*chronos*) all his abusive ways and become glorified in heaven (*kairos*) so he could speak to her as she'd always wanted, as a pure Nurturing energy. She traded places, role-playing her idealized father and speaking to her imagined Child self. A childhood wound healed (*kairos*). There was no doubt left in anyone's mind that we were in the presence of Divine Love. Awesome! Everyone present was uplifted and inspired.

In Exercise 14 Then and Now Parents, you recalled some painful childhood memories. In the following exercise, you will do more than recall a memory. Instead of your mind recalling a painful memory, your body will find it. It may or may not be one you recalled earlier. Trust your body and give it the authority to find the memory it needs you to address.

Note: The mind won't let us remember more than we can manage. Please treat with respect and gentleness the potentially vulnerable material the following exercise brings up for many people. Seeing a Spiritual leader or a therapist may give additional support in dealing with very painful memories.

Exercise 16: Evoking a Painful Childhood Memory

Step 1: Record the following directions or have a friend read them while you do the exercise. Your body sensations and then emotions, not your mind, are the road to the memory. When the Child accepts your gift, there needs to be a physiological change in the young self that is felt in your real body, a release of tension somewhere. Only a change in the Nurturer changes the Child, so don't try to persuade or convince the Child to change. Love yourself more than you have ever loved anyone else, even your mother. With body-felt compassion, accept the Child as he or she is. Read aloud and record the beginning with Step 2: B and ending with Step 5: D. Don't record the note after 4 A.

Step 2:

A. Find a comfortable place where you can sit in an upright position with your back supported. Have your tablet, pencil, drawing pad, and crayons nearby.
B. Close your eyes and direct your attention to your breath, breathing in through your nose and out through your mouth. (Pause.) Notice the sensations your breath creates in your nose and throat. (Pause.) Expand your chest with your breath as you relax your belly. Breathe in and out until your body, breath, and thoughts become as one and you feel soft and blended. If this exercise is

difficult, repeat your name until you can achieve these results. (Pause.)

C. Begin to count down from ten, nine, eight ... (Take a long pause.) (two, one), becoming more relaxed with each thought, allowing your chin to rest comfortably on your chest and your jaw to drop. (Pause) Imagine that you arrive in the very core of yourself. Notice what you see and how you feel in this place, allowing any images that arise to get your attention ... Accept all your images and feelings without trying to figure them out. (Pause.)

D. Find a memory when your younger self needed care. (Pause.) Find a younger time when you had this feeling ... and a time before that. Trace the feeling back into time until your youngest age when this particular sensation was present.

E. Observe this young part of yourself. Identify the physical and behavioral manifestations of the Child up to six years old. (Pause.) Notice the age of the Child, the position of the body, the feeling communicated ... Mad? ... Sad? ... or ... afraid?

F. Now, imagine that you move into the body of your Child self. You have little hands, ... little feet ... And you're looking out of little eyes. (Pause ten seconds.) See what you can see ... Hear what you can hear ... And feel what you can feel. (Pause fifteen to twenty seconds.)

Step 3:

A. Now imagine that you move back from the Child and Nurturer and into the part of you who traveled down to this place, your Mentor. From this perspective, see your Nurturer and Wounded Child as separate images. They may move together, speak to each other, explore as they stay in contact, and relate to each other. (Pause five seconds.)

B. Make this memory into a slide ... and view it from a distance. Push it into the distance. Your Mentor views the picture and decides what the Child really wants.

1. understanding (being heard or listened to)
2. stimulation (actively engaged)
3. recognition (positive attention, validation)
4. security (boundaries)
5. companionship (togetherness)
6. information (instructions or teachings)
7. freedom of imagination without judgment, shame, or criticism

Step 4:

A. Now, switch perspective and move back into your nurturing self. Be in your nurturing body, mind-set, and feeling. (Pause ten seconds.) Be an ally from the future. Communicate *acceptance* of your Child self even if the Child won't speak or even look at you. It will in time. Accept the Child as is—silent. Offer the Wounded Child what has been missing all these years. (Pause ten seconds.) Place your gift in an object to symbolize what is given and leave it in the Child's presence. Thank your inner Child for being present with you and assure it you will return, giving a specific day, time, and duration.

Note: In other words, make an appointment with yourself for ten minutes on Tuesday at 9:00 a.m. At the appointed time, you will repeat this exercise. Each time will reveal more and more information about what you need to be whole. Remember, the Child part always gets its needs met in both *chronos* and *kairos* time, and it always has the last word. How about that!

    B. Whenever you're ready, hold your young self in your hand and allow it to become smaller and smaller as you become bigger and bigger. Then put your Child in your heart by placing your hand on your chest.

    C. Begin to count yourself up—one, two, three … nine, and ten. Once again, you're sitting with your back straight and your head level. When you're ready, open your eyes.

Step 5:

    A. Make a drawing of your Child self. Write a story, poem, or dialogue about you and your Child.

    B. Make a note of your experience, noting the details of what you saw, heard, and felt. Note what was missing from the scene that would make what you saw, heard, and felt complete. When you repeat this exercise, provide the missing part. Allow the feeling … Feel completion and satisfaction in your body. Carry this feeling with you.

    C. Take the imagined gift and then make it present in your reality. This act will demonstrate your integrity and ability to act responsibly as an adult toward you as a Child.

Explosive Layer

At this point, we have peeled five layers of our metaphoric onion mentioned in Step 1.

1. phony level: We behave as if, not as, we are.
2. phobic layer: Objection (fear) of being what we are, resistance
3. impasse: What is behind the objection, the feeling of being dead, of disappearing? (Answer is reached through a trance state. When we become aware of the impasse, it will collapse.)
4. implosive: Stored energy to arrive at the fifth layer in our progression to becoming authentic
5. explosive: Implosive state is dissolved into one of four types: joy, grief, anger, or orgasm.

How we relate to time and eventually our upcoming death is the crucial element in our self-actualization and our relationship with others. Our implosive state of internal turmoil, pain, and tension are from our Critic as it tries to negotiate the ending of chronological time (death), and from our wounded Child as it seeks to join the Spiritual truth of eternal existence (*kairos*). Our pain announces the impasse between reason and faith. Religious circles refer to this internal conflict as "being under God's conviction." Evidence of a successful journey through this impasse and the implosive layer of our imagined death to the completion of the explosive layer is always a body-felt experience.

The explosive layer releases with a surge of excitement felt in our bodies in *chronos* time. This is our surrender to death and acceptance of everlasting life; tension from our resistance to the death of the chronological moment releases, and excitement rushes in to fill the empty space as we allow acceptance of our Spiritual rebirth into our spiritual self. (And sometimes we even get goose bumps.)

Our extraordinary Divine Child, once hidden to survive (like Moses and Jesus) and threatened since birth by the Critic through our rejecting, projecting, and deflecting the love that is our birthright, is no longer hidden or unaware. Now our deified Nurturer protects our Divine Child. The Divine Child recognizes its own worth (Wounded Child healed) and takes its rightful place (infinite Divine Innocence), providing unprecedented opportunity for spontaneity, imagination, creativity, and Spirituality.

Pledge to Self

I will not destroy that which I have created from my youth [Critic] to aid me in the world, but I will treat it kindly by rejecting it with love [Nurturer]. As Jesus [Nurturer] employed the love of God to dispel darkness, so too will I use the love of God to rebuke my negative judgmental voices [Critic] and become as a little child [Divine Child] receiving my birthright the love the world has denied me so I may receive the promise of becoming one with the infinite. Then I can enter the kingdom of heaven, completing my transcendence.

Congratulations for deciding to choose perseverance, hope, and happiness. Continue to push forward from good to great. Go in love and peace. Soar with your Soul.

APPENDIX

Characteristic Checklist

Mentor

____Is unemotional

____Contains factual data

____Contains accumulated beliefs and values (even those contradictory, outdated, or magical)

____Knows the positive intent of other internal dialoguing parts

____Is constructive

Critic (Destructive)

____Is incapable of love

____Can appear suddenly

____Talks when we attempt to be silent, when we are asleep, and when we are in conversation

____Has many faces and voices

____Can sound like a male or female and be sweet or cruel

____Lies, cheats, and manipulates

____Creates personal suffering to get its way

____Intends to gain recognition and remain important

Divine Nurturer (Instructive)

_____Is unconditionally loving

_____Is peaceful, intuitive

_____Is accepting and protective

_____Is forgiving and nonjudgmental

Divine Child

_____Is ceaselessly creative

_____Finds a sense of value present in everything

_____Is spontaneous

_____Is the source of all basic emotions

All Children's Primary Needs

- understanding (being heard or listened to)
- stimulation (active engagement)
- recognition (positive attention, validation)
- security (boundaries, food, shelter)
- companionship (togetherness)
- information (instructions or teachings)
- freedom of imagination without judgment, shame, or criticism

Your Internal Nurturer

- listens to, acknowledges, and accepts child's feelings;
- accepts and treats child with respect as is;
- gives specific honest praise about something specific;
- uses *I* messages rather than *you* messages;
- involves the Child (Divine Child) in problem solving and decision making that is relative to both the Nurturer and Child; and
- respects feelings, needs, wants, suggestions, and wisdom.

Self-Test

The following statements carry an inference and can be placed in one of the four mental categories—Mentor, Critic, Nurturer, Child. Check yourself on how well you can recognize these. (Statements in parentheses imply meaning through tone of voice.)

1. "If I have told you once ..." (Stupid!)
2. "Don't get smart with me!" (Be obedient.)
3. "Don't be a pill." (You're bitter, difficult.)
4. "That isn't a face I would advise you to make." (Hide yourself.)
5. "Look at me when I'm talking to you." (Override your instinct.)
6. "If I wanted to know your opinion, I'd ask for it." (What you think has no value.)
7. "You'd lose your head if it weren't screwed on." (You can't take care of yourself.)
8. "Whistle before breakfast; cry before noon." (Waking up happy means trouble.)
9. "If you bite your nails, it shows you're boy crazy." (Actions: self-revealing meaning)
10. "All men are the same. They just have different faces so you can tell them apart." (Discount the opposite sex or self, if male.)
11. "You aren't going out like that, are you?" (You look terrible.)
12. "Don't you think people look at the back of your hair, too?" (Pay attention.)

13. "Your hair isn't clean until it squeaks." (So be thorough and listen.)
14. "You're only as old as you feel." (Feel good or young.)
15. "A quitter never wins; a winner never quits." (Success is more important than feelings.)
16. "There is a place for everything and everything in its place." (Neatness is valued.)
17. "One step at a time is all it takes to get there. (Value the present moment.)
18. "I'll write a poem." (Free expression)
19. "The way you are pleases me." (You're okay.)
20. "When I die, you can go with me." (I will never leave you.)

Answers

Critical: 1–7, 11, 12 (Critic)
Intellectual: 8–10, 13–18 (Mentor)
Creative: 18 (Child)
Loving: 19–20 (Nurturer)

PROGRESSION TO BECOMING AUTHENTIC
(LAYERS OF THE ONION)

1. phony level: We behave as if, not as, we are.
2. phobic layer: Objection (fear) of being what we are, resistance
3. impasse: What is behind the objection, the feeling of being dead, of disappearing? (Answer is reached through a trance state. When we become aware of the impasse, it will collapse.)
4. implosive: Stored energy
5. explosive: Implosive state is dissolved into one of four types: joy, grief, anger, or orgasm.

Strategies Preventing Progression

- introjection—to incorporate information into one's personality unconsciously without contemplation or analyses
- projection—disowned attributes of ourselves (attitudes, ideas, feelings) that are assigned to others
- retroflection—substituting ourselves for the object of our own actions
- deflection—process of distracting ourselves so that we can avoid contact with our environment
- confluence—giving over our creative energy to others, passively going along

Works Cited

Abrams, Jeremiah. *Reclaiming the Inner Child*. Los Angeles: Jeremy P. Tarcher, 1990.

Bandier, Richard, and John Grinder. *Reframing*. Moab, UT: Human Science Press, 1988.

Biffle, Christopher. *A Journey through Childhood*. Los Angeles: Jeremy P. Tarcher, 1989.

Blantner, Adam, and Allee Blatner. *The Art of Play*. New York: Human Science Press, 1988.

Bradshaw, John. *Healing the Shame That Binds You*. Deerfield Beach, FL: Health Communications, 1988.

Brandon, Nathaniel. *Honoring the Self*. Los Angeles: Jeremy P. Tarcher, 1983.

Chopra, Deepak. *The Seven Spiritual Laws of Success*. San Rafael, CA: Amber-Allen Publishing and New World Library, 1994.

Davis, Bruce, and Genny Wright Davis. *The Magical Child within You*. Berkley, CA: Celestial Arts, 1950.

Dinkmeryer, Don, and Gary D. McKay. *The Parent's Handbook*. Circle Pines, MN: American Guidance Service, 1988.

Fisher, Roger, William Ury, and Bruce Patton. *Getting to Yes, Negotiating Agreements without Giving in*. Westminster, London: Penguin Group, 1991.

Friel, John, and Linda Friel. *Adult Children :the Secrets of Dysfunctional Families*. Dearfield Beach, FL: Health Communications, 1988.

Geering, Lloyd. *The World of Relation: An Introduction to Martin Buber's I and Thou*. Kelburn Wellington, New Zealand: Victoria University Press, 1983.

Heckler, Richard Strozzi. *The Anatomy of Change.* Berkeley, CA: North Atlantic Books, 1993.

Helmstetter, Shad. *What to Say When You Talk to Your Self.* New York: Simon and Schuster, 1963.

Jacobson, Sid. *Meta-cation.* Cupertino, CA: Meta Publications, 1983.

Jampolsky, Gerald G. *Love Is Letting Go of Fear.* New York: Bantam Books, 1979.

Kirsten, Grace, and Richard Robertiello. *Big You and Little You, Separation Therapy.* New York: Dial Press, 1977.

Larsen, Earnie. *Old Patterns, New Truths.* New York: Harper and Row, 1988.

Lipton, Bruce H. *The Biology of Belief.* Carlsbad, CA: Hay House, 2008.

Margulies, Alfred. *The Empathic Imagination.* New York: W.W. Norton & Company, 1989.

Missildine, W. Hugh. *Your Inner Child of the Past.* New York: Simon and Schuster, 1963.

May, Rollo. *Love and Will.* New York: W. W. Norton & Company, 1969.

Oaklander, Violet. *Windows to our Children.* Moab, UT: Real People Press, 1978.

Pollard III, John K. *Self-Parenting.* Malibu, CA: Generic Human Studies Publishing, 1961.

Porterfield, Kay. *Violent Voices.* Deerfield Beach, FL: Health Communications, 1989.

Sanford, John A. *Healing and Wholeness.* Mahwah, NJ: Paulist Press, 1977.

Sanford, John A. *The Kingdom Within: The Inner Meaning of Jesus' Sayings.* New York: Harper Collins, 1987.

Schiffman, Muriel. *Gestalt Self.* Berkeley, CA: Wingbow, 1971.

Shealy, Norman C. *Living Bliss.* Carlsbad, CA: Hay House, 2014.

Steindl-Rast, David. *A Listening Heart.* New York: Crossroad, 1988.

Tollel, Eckhart. *The Power of Now: A Guide to Spiritual Enlightenment.* Novato, CA: New World Library, 2004.

Weinberg, George. *The Heart of Psychotherapy: A Journey into the Mind and Office of a Therapist at Work.* New York: St. Martin's Press, 1984, reprinted 1996.

Whitfield, Charles L. *Healing the Child Within.* Pompano Beach, FL: Health Communications, 1987.

Zi, Nancy. *The Art of Breathing.* San Francisco: Bantam Books, 1986.

Zukav, Gary. *The Seat of the Soul.* New York: Fireside, Simon and Schuster, 1990.

VIDEOS

Using Your Creative Brain. Educational Dimensions Group. VHS video. Stanford, Conn. The Group, 1985.

Healing Mind, Healing Practice. Herbert, Benson. Harvard Medical School. Department of Continuing Education.; Harvard Medical School. Mind/Body Medical Institute.; Templeton Foundation.; Reunion Productions. VHS tape Boston, MA. The Institute, 1996.

FOR YOUR PROTECTION

Janice McDermott, M.Ed, LCSW, provides seminarian instruction in the use of the model *A Sacred Trust: The Inner Child*, as described in this writing. These seminars don't give certification to teach. At present, there are no authorized or qualified instructors, but you can become one.

A six-hour Personal Growth Experience is offered in a small-group setting throughout the year. To participate in a Personal Growth Seminar, Individual Training, or to cosponsor a seminar, please contact the following:

McDermott Seminars & Training
114 Rue St. Germaine
Carriere, MS 39426
e-mail: jmac9087@att.net

Printed in the United States
By Bookmasters